ANIMAL WATCH

A Visual Introduction to

SHARKS

SKATES AND RAYS

Sharks: A Visual Introduction to Sharks, Skates and Rays
Copyright © 1999 AND Cartographic Publishers Ltd
http://www.and.nl
Created and Packaged by Firecrest Books Ltd. in association
with AND Cartographic Publishers Ltd.

Checkmark Books
An imprint of Facts On File, Inc.
11 Penn Plaza
New York NY 10001

Library of Congress Cataloging-in-Publication Data
Stonehouse, Bernard.
A visual introduction to sharks/Bernard Stonehouse:
illustrated by Martin Camm.
p. cm. — (Animal watch)
Includes index..
Summary: In text and pictures, describes the various
kinds of sharks, their life cycles, and the
best locations for humans to see them.
ISBN 0-8160-3924-0
1. Sharks — Juvenile literature. [1. Sharks] I. Camm, Martin,
ill. II. Title. III. Series: Stonehouse, Bernard. Animal Watch.
QL638.9.S8497 1999
597.3—dc21 99-10219

Checkmark Books are available at special discounts when
purchased in bulk quantities for businesses, associations,
institutions or sales promotions. Please call our Special Sales
Department in New York at (212) 967-8800 or (800) 322-8755.

You can find Facts On File on the World Wide Web at
http://www.factsonfile.com

CONTENTS

FACT FILE
GREAT WHITE SHARK

Order:	Lamniformes
Family:	Carchariidae
Latin name:	*Carcharadon carcharias*
Color:	Pale gray or blue above, white underside
Length:	Up to 20 ft (6 m)
Habitat:	Surface waters in cool tropical, subtropical and warm temperate seas
Range:	Worldwide

(For more information on great white sharks see pages 32–33)

WHAT IS A SHARK?

How sharks are different from bony fish and how they are adapted for different kinds of life in the sea.

WHAT ARE SHARKS?

Sharks are fish, but quite different from most of the fish that we see in rivers and ponds, or catch for food in the sea. The biggest difference is in their skeleton. Shark skeletons are made of cartilage (gristle) rather than bone. (You can read more about that on pages 10–11). There are many other differences, some of which seem to date back a very long time—300 million years or more—in their history.

So we think of sharks as in some ways more "primitive" than bony fish. There are fewer different kinds alive today than there have been in the past, and nowhere near so many kinds as there are of bony fish. (How many different kinds of bony fish? About 12,000 have been discovered so far, and there are probably more undiscovered.)

However, sharks swim, hunt, catch their food and in many other ways work just as well and efficiently as bony fish.

THIS GREAT WHITE SHARK is everyone's idea of a big, fierce shark. It lives in tropical and temperate waters, usually near coasts, swimming in shallow waters where it hunts mainly for fish. Also known as the white shark or blue shark, it comes in a range of dull tones that match the colors of the sea. This makes it hard to see from above or the side. Similarly, the pale white or yellowish undersurface is difficult to see from beneath, against a bright sky. So this big shark, up to 20 ft (6 m) long, can swim quietly and almost invisibly through the water in search of its prey.

As in most sharks, the head is blunt, the eyes are well forward, the nostrils deep set. The underslung jaw is armed with several rows of very sharp teeth. The body, sleek, slender and streamlined, tapers away to a tail with upper and lower lobes. As in most sharks, the upper lobe is larger and stronger than the lower. The tail and rear half of the body, packed with solid muscle, form the propeller that drives the shark forward through the water.

Most sharks have five large gill slits on either side, with a smaller extra slit, the "spiracle," in front of them. There is usually a big central dorsal fin, visible when the shark is swimming near the surface, with smaller fins top (dorsal) and below (anal) close to the tail. The two pairs of movable fins along the sides of the body correspond to the arms and legs of a reptile or mammal, and are used for steering.

Great white shark

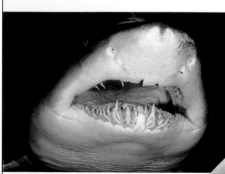

Several rows of sharp, cutting teeth, constantly being replaced

Where do we find them?

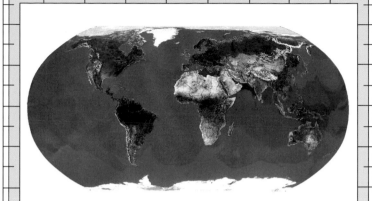

Most sharks have five gill slits, like this reef shark

MANY NAMES

Sharks that range widely over the oceans, and make themselves well known in several different places, often acquire several different names. The great white shark is also called "white pointer," "white shark" and "blue shark" in different parts of its range. Some Australians call it "white death."

These common names are confusing enough, but even the scientists who study sharks often have trouble deciding whether the big sharks that are called "great white sharks" in Australian waters are of the same species as similar large, pale-colored sharks off South Africa and South America. So sharks of the same species may be given several Latin names by different scientists.

SHARKS OF ALL KINDS

Most of us think of sharks as huge, fierce, dangerous monsters that live in warm oceans and attack people when they go for a swim. Some sharks are just like that. The great white shark illustrated on these pages, for example, grows to two to three times the length of a human. And sharks as big as this have attacked and killed swimmers in warm, shallow waters off coasts as far apart as Australia, California, Italy and England.

However, there are more than 350 species (different kinds) of sharks. Though nearly all of them are hunters and meat-eaters, they are mostly small, much smaller than fully grown humans. They are also rather timid, especially when people are about. Most of the smaller sharks feed on small fish, squid and other creatures that live on or near the seabed. Only a few of the bigger ones—like this great white shark—are big enough to attack large fish, which is what they mainly live on. Very few are big enough to attack people.

Sharks and their close relatives, the skates and rays, live in all the world's oceans, from warm tropical to icy polar seas. Some species stay entirely in warm water, others migrate annually from warm to cooler waters, in other words, they move around, living in a wide range of sea temperatures. A few species move easily from the sea to rivers and lakes. (Read more about this on pages 36-37.)

Streamlined and built for speed: silky shark looking for a meal

WHERE CAN WE SEE THEM?

Unlike whales and dolphins, sharks tend to be shy and stay away from boats and people. Still, they are always hungry and can be attracted by food. So fishermen who know where to find sharks take passengers out in their boats and throw dead fish, meat or other food over the side. After a few minutes the sharks smell the food and gather round to sample it.

Easiest to find in temperate waters are basking sharks (pages 28-29), which are among the biggest and gentlest and live close to the surface. These come back each year to the same areas offshore, to feed on plankton and small fish. When they are around, the local fishermen usually know just where to find them.

Some kinds of sharks live well in aquariums and marine parks like SeaWorld. If they have clean water and plenty of space for swimming, you can often see them there behaving much as they would in the sea outside.

Divers off the Bahamas watching sharks being fed

SHARKS AND THEIR RELATIONS

Sharks—giants and hunters of the oceans and, with their relations the rays and skates, monsters of the seabed.

VERTEBRATES

Fish belong to the group of animals called "vertebrates," which means that they have backbones made up of blocks called vertebrae. Also included in the group are amphibians (for example, frogs and salamanders), reptiles (turtles, crocodiles), birds and mammals, including man.

Biologists believe that all the vertebrates evolved from ancestors that lived in the sea. They must have swum and looked very much like fish, with fins and tail for swimming and gills for breathing.

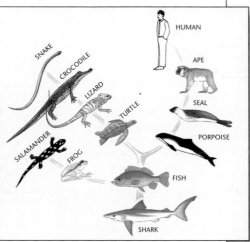

Some of the many different kinds of vertebrates

CARTILAGE, OR GRISTLE

Sharks and their near relations have skeletons made, not of bone, but of cartilage, which is softer, lighter and more springy than bone. Another name for it is "gristle." All young vertebrates, such as humans, have a lot of cartilage in their skeletons while they are growing. As we grow to full size, we replace most of it with bone, keeping bits of it as cartilage in the ridge of our nose, our ears, breastbone, and ends of ribs.

The sharks and their kin have cartilage all over—in their skulls, backbones, ribs, fins and everywhere else where skeleton or stiffening is needed. In big sharks, some of the gristle—for example, in the vertebrae—is strengthened by calcification (adding bony plates), but never enough to make true bones. Fishes that keep their cartilage throughout life are grouped in the class Chondrichthyes (pronounce it kon-**drik**-thy-eeze).

A T FIRST GLANCE, sharks look like typical fishes—long, streamlined, with rounded head, slender tail, smooth or scaly surface, two pairs of fins, and one or two fins along their backs. However, they all belong to the special group of fishes called Chondrichthyes, or gristle fish, that have cartilage, or gristle, in their skeletons instead of bone.

Sharks are the best known of all the gristle fish, mainly because some of them are big enough and strong enough to be man-eaters. In fact, only a few species of sharks ever hunt humans. Most kinds of sharks never grow bigger than 3.4 ft (1 m) long.

entirely on plankton (tiny floating plants and animals) and small fish.

The smallest sharks, called cookie-cutter sharks, are less than 1 ft (30 cm) long when fully grown. They sometimes bite and hold onto bigger fishes, leaving a scar shaped like a cookie or biscuit.

Gristle fish include rays and skates also. They are related to sharks but look quite different. Most of them live on the sea bottom and are flattened as though they have been run over.

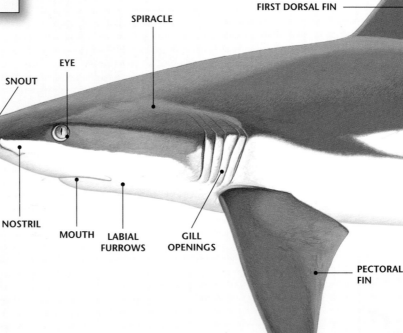

Nearly all sharks, including the fiercest man-eaters, spend most of their time hunting fish or browsing on the seabed.

The biggest of all sharks are whale sharks, which grow to as much as 40 ft (12 m) long. Next biggest are basking sharks, which grow to as long as 33 ft (10 m). (See pages 28–29.) Though enormous, these are among the laziest and least fierce of all the sharks. They swim slowly in surface waters, feeding almost

The biggest are more than 10 ft (3 m) long, the smallest less than 1.6 ft (50 cm) when fully grown. Though most are harmless to humans, some have sharp spines that inject poison if you walk on them, and others give strong electric shocks if you try to catch them or touch them accidentally. (You can read more about these strange fishes on pages 40–41.)

Different kinds of fishes

Teeth of sand tiger shark, growing on a jaw of tough gristle

HOW STRONG IS GRISTLE?

Gristle is softer than bone and not so firm. So having a skeleton made of gristle instead of bone may sound like a weakness. Can these gristle fish become as big and strong as bony fish? Certainly they are as big, and even bigger. Whale sharks and basking sharks (see main text), the world's biggest fish, are both gristle fish. Many of the smaller sharks are strong enough to hunt and tear to pieces bony fish, like tuna and marlin, that are as big as themselves.

Apart from their skeletons, cartilaginous and bony fishes differ in several ways:

BONY FISHES:
- Surface covered with smooth skin or scales, usually slimy
- Gills covered by hinged plate (operculum)
- Tail with two symmetrical lobes
- Fins spiny
- Mouth edged with lips, made up of several small plates
- Produce many small eggs

CARTILAGINOUS FISHES:
- Surface covered with tiny denticles; feels rough like sandpaper
- Gills open, usually five or six on either side
- Tail with big upper lobe, smaller lower lobe
- Fins fleshy, with spiny edges
- Mouth edged with skin, usually covered with teeth
- Produce a few large eggs or live young

Goldfish (bony)

Spotted catfish (cartilaginous)

BONY AND CARTILAGINOUS FISHES

There are many thousands of different kinds of fishes. Biologists divide the living fishes of the world into five major groups (called "classes"), according to their skeletons and other characteristics.

Most of the common fishes (for example, cod, mackerel, pike, trout) have skeletons made of hard bone, as hard as the bones in a human arm or leg. You can see some of their bones when you eat these kinds of fishes. Often you need to be careful not to swallow the smaller, spiny ones. Bony fishes are all grouped together in the class Actinopterygii (pronounce it ak-tin-op-ter-**ijee**-eye)

THE CARTILAGINOUS FISHES
The two main groups of cartilaginous fishes are

SHARKS:
Mostly fast-swimming hunters, including man-eaters, living at all depths of the sea, a few in fresh-water. About 350 different kinds.

Thresher shark

Angel shark

RAYS AND SKATES:
Mostly flat fish, living on the seabed, though some live at the surface or in mid-water. About 300 different kinds.

SECOND DORSAL FIN

PRECAUDAL PIT

CAUDAL FIN

CLASPER (MALE)

CAUDAL KEEL

ANAL FIN

PELVIC FIN

The gristle in the skeleton is reinforced and bound with strands of much stronger material, of the kind that holds our own bones and joints together, and with strands or plates of bone. Gristle is not as heavy as bone, so gristle fish tend to weigh less than bony fish of the same size.

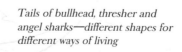

Tails of bullhead, thresher and angel sharks—different shapes for different ways of living

IDENTIFYING SHARKS

Except for the very big, slow-moving ones, live sharks are not easy to identify, especially if they are in the water and swimming fast. If you see a recently dead shark lying on the beach, you can usually say which major group (order) it belongs to, simply by noting the arrangement of dorsal and anal fins, and a few other small points. This key may help:

A *Has it an anal fin below the tail?*
If NO, go to **B**
If YES, go to **C**

B *No anal fin. Has it ...*
■ *a flattened body like a ray?*
Squatiniformes
(angel sharks)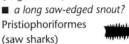
■ *a long saw-edged snout?*
Pristiophoriformes
(saw sharks)
■ *a short snout without saws?*
Squaliformes
(dogfish sharks)

C *Anal fin present. How many dorsal fins?*
If ONE, go to **D**. If TWO, go to **E**

D *One dorsal fin* Hexanchiformes
(6-gilled, 7-gilled
and frilled sharks)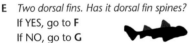

E *Two dorsal fins. Has it dorsal fin spines?*
If YES, go to **F**
If NO, go to **G**

F *Dorsal fin spines present*
Heterodontiformes
(bullhead sharks)

G *No dorsal fin spines. Has it a small mouth with nostril grooves?*
If YES, go to **H**. If NO, go to **I**

H *Small mouth with nostril grooves*
Orectilobiformes
(carpet sharks
and their kin)

I *Large mouth, no nostril grooves. Has it a third eyelid?*
If YES, go to **J**
If NO, go to **K**

J *Third eyelid present*
Carcharhiniformes
(ground sharks)

K *Third eyelid absent* Lamniformes
(mackerel sharks
and their kin)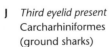

THESE ARE THE SHARKS

Fast and slow, big and small, gentle and fierce, the 350 kinds of sharks may be grouped into eight families.

FISH BIOLOGISTS block the 350 species of sharks into 30 "families," and the families into eight bigger groups called "orders," which are shown here. Species contained in a family are thought to be closely related—that is, to have evolved from a common ancestor many millions of years ago. Similarly, families in each order are believed to be closely related to each other.

Three of the orders contain only one family each. Members of each are specialized for particular ways of life on the seabed and are quite unlike other sharks. One order has five species, in two families, again with characteristics that distinguish them from all other sharks.

The remaining four orders are bigger, each containing between three and eight families, again all with slightly different characteristics. The largest order, the Carchariniformes, contains well over half the living species of sharks.

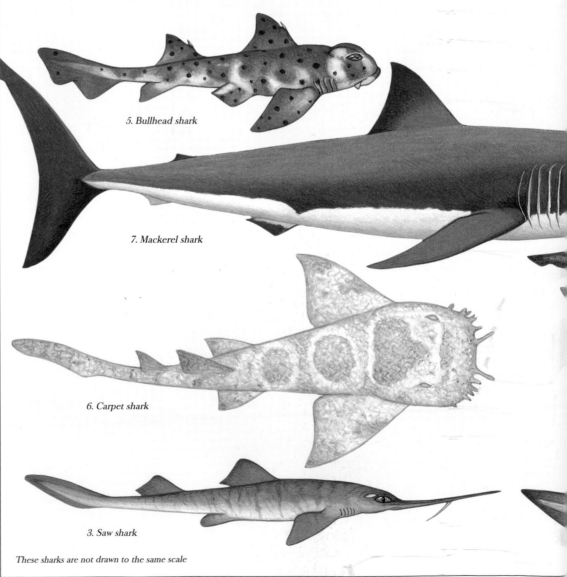

5. Bullhead shark

7. Mackerel shark

6. Carpet shark

3. Saw shark

These sharks are not drawn to the same scale

1. OLD SHARKS
Order Hexanchiformes (pronounce it Hex-an-ki-form-ees)

Two small families, the six-gilled and seven-gilled sharks (two species of each), and the frilled sharks (one species). These are primitive sharks, little changed over many millions of years. They have only one dorsal fin, with an anal fin immediately below it, and either six or seven gill slits, whereas most other sharks have five. They live mostly in cool or temperate deep water.

2. BRAMBLE, ROUGH AND DOGFISH SHARKS
Order Squaliformes (pronounce it Skwa-li-form-ees)

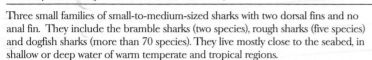

Three small families of small-to-medium-sized sharks with two dorsal fins and no anal fin. They include the bramble sharks (two species), rough sharks (five species) and dogfish sharks (more than 70 species). They live mostly close to the seabed, in shallow or deep water of warm temperate and tropical regions.

3. SAW SHARKS
Order Pristiophoriformes (pronounce it Pristi-oh-fori-form-ees)

This order contains only one family, with only five species. Saw sharks are mostly around 3.3 ft (1 m) long, with two dorsal fins and no anal fin. They are the only sharks with a distinctive long snout, which has teeth ranged on either edge like a double-edged saw. You find them mainly in warm seas, living on the bottom in shallow or moderately deep water.

4. ANGEL SHARKS
Order Squatiniformes (pronounce it Skwat-eye-ni-form-ees)

Another small order with about 13 species, all in a single family. These are squat, lumpy fish, some more than 6.5 ft (2 m) long, flattened like rays, with two dorsal fins and no anal fin. They live mainly in warm seas, on the seabed in shallow to moderately deep water.

5. BULLHEAD SHARKS
Order Heterodontiformes (pronounce it Het-ero-donti-form-ees)

A single-family order, with eight species so far identified. These are squat, powerful-looking sharks with a square-cut head that grow to about 4–5 ft (1.5 m). They have two dorsal fins, each with a thick spine embedded in its leading edge, and an anal fin. Bullhead sharks live on the seabed, mainly in shallow tropical or temperate water.

6. CARPET SHARKS
Order Orectolobiformes (pronounce it O-recto-low-bi-form-ees)

A large, mixed group of 33 species divided among seven families, including wobbegongs, blind sharks, carpet sharks, whale sharks and nurse sharks. They live mainly in warm tropical waters, and several that live on the seabed are patterned, colored or fringed with barbels (fleshy fingers)—hence the name "carpet sharks." They carry two dorsal fins and an anal fin, and the nostrils have barbels and deep grooves that run into the upper corners of the mouth. Though most live on the sand, mud and reefs of the seabed, this group also includes the whale sharks, which live entirely at the ocean surface.

7. MACKEREL SHARKS
Order Lamniformes (pronounce it Lam-ni-form-ees)

This is a large group of mainly large, surface-living sharks, including mackerel sharks, basking sharks, goblin sharks, megamouth sharks, thresher sharks and mako sharks—15 species in all, spread among seven families. They range from shallow down to deep water in warm and temperate oceans. Most are long and powerfully built, with two dorsal fins and an anal fin, and often a long or extended snout. Several species are known to be man-eaters.

8. GROUND SHARKS
Order Carcharhiniformes (pronounce it Car-cha-rye-ni-form-ees)

This is by far the biggest order of sharks, made up of almost 200 species, divided into eight families. With two dorsal fins and an anal fin, they also have "nictitating" (movable) lower eyelids, so are the only sharks that can even half-close their eyes. The collective name "ground sharks" describes many of them that live in coastal waters, on or near the seabed, including the nine species of hammerhead sharks with their extraordinary flattened heads. However, carcharine sharks also include more than 40 species of swift, surface-living requiem sharks, some of which live in the open ocean far from land.

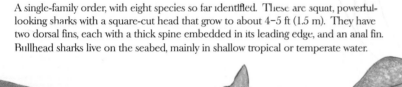

1. Old shark

2. Bramble shark

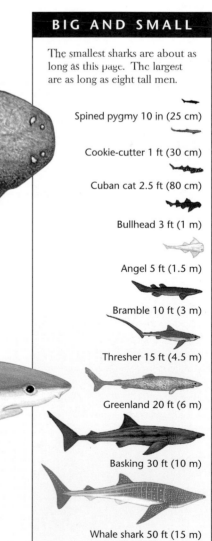

4. Angel shark

8. Ground shark

BIG AND SMALL

The smallest sharks are about as long as this page. The largest are as long as eight tall men.

Spined pygmy 10 in (25 cm)

Cookie-cutter 1 ft (30 cm)

Cuban cat 2.5 ft (80 cm)

Bullhead 3 ft (1 m)

Angel 5 ft (1.5 m)

Bramble 10 ft (3 m)

Thresher 15 ft (4.5 m)

Greenland 20 ft (6 m)

Basking 30 ft (10 m)

Whale shark 50 ft (15 m)

SWIMMING

Like other fishes, sharks swim forward by moving their tail and rear end of their body from side to side. The big central dorsal fin keeps the front and middle of the body from moving sideways. The shark's weight tends to push the nose downward, but the upward tilt of the snout and the front fins lift the front end as the shark moves forward.

FAST AND SLOW

Sharks that swim fast keep their body stiff, like an arrow or torpedo. Slower-moving ones are more flexible, throwing themselves into S-bends. Fast swimmers move almost constantly to draw enough oxygen from the water flowing past their gills. Slower, lazy ones use far less energy and less oxygen, and take long rests between spells of swimming.

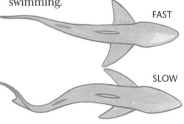

FAST

SLOW

HOW FAST?

Fast-swimming sharks, such as great whites and bronze whalers, swim at more than 30 mph (50 km/h), faster than most whales and dolphins. But for much of the time they probably swim at half these speeds or less. Over long distances they travel 40 miles (60 km) or more per day.

Bronze whaler shark—one of the fastest-moving sharks

HOW SHARKS WORK

Swimming, breathing, hunting—sharks come in different shapes and sizes, adapted for their different ways of life in the seas of the world.

ALL SHARKS ARE SLIGHTLY DENSER than the water in which they swim (see "Buoyancy," on opposite page). The densest are those that live on or near the seabed, where their weight helps to keep them down. Those that live in mid-water or near the surface have a big liver, full of oil, which makes them less dense than the bottom-living forms. They tend to sink slowly when at rest, but need only to swim very gently forward to overcome it. The forward movement lifts their front end enough to push them slightly upward.

How sharks work

BUOYANCY

Like a shark, when you float in the sea, you are slightly denser than the water around you. So, if you do nothing, you tend to sink. You can reduce your density by taking in a lungful of air, which helps to keep you afloat. Let the air out, and you start to sink again. Some bony fish have a balloon of air inside them that reduces their density in this way, but sharks do not.

Many sharks have a big liver full of oil that is much less dense than water. This reduces their overall density, much as a life jacket, or a piece of polystyrene tucked under your belt, reduces your overall density and keeps you afloat. To stay up in the water without a life jacket, all you have to do is swim very gently, pressing the water down with your cupped hands or feet. That is all a shark has to do. A very slight movement forward pushes the water down and the shark up, enough to keep it level at any depth.

SENSES

Nearly all sharks have a good sense of smell (or combined taste and smell) and hunt by sensing the water. They can detect fish or human blood in very tiny concentrations. Through their "lateral line" system—tiny receptors in the skin of head and flanks—they can detect vibrations and movement a long way away. Some sharks, especially those that hunt at the surface, have very keen eyesight. Those that live in muddy or deep water have to rely on smell, vibrations and small electric currents for hunting (see page 39).

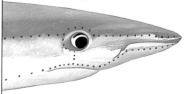

Eyes and lines of sensory organs help a shark to find its food

BREATHING

Sharks swim with the mouth open, taking in water, which rushes past the gills and is forced out through the gill slits. On the way, the gills extract oxygen from the water and pass it into the bloodstream, at the same time ridding the body of carbon dioxide, a waste product.

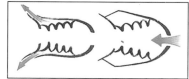

Water enters the mouth and passes out through the gills

SKIN

Most sharks are covered not with flat scales like bony fishes, but with thousands of tiny "'denticles" (little teeth). Each denticle is made of a very hard, bony substance that grows just like a tooth. And denticles, like the teeth, are constantly replaced. The underlying skin is tough and leathery, so sharks are very well protected from bites by other animals. Dried shark's skin, called "shagreen," can be used like sandpaper to smooth wood.

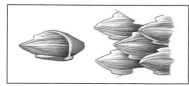

Denticles—tiny toothlike scales

BREEDING

Most sharks have a breeding season, when the male organs (testes) inside the body start to produce sperm, and the female organs (ovaries) produce eggs. Males have "claspers"—pointed rods on their pelvic fins. At the mating season, males and females pair, and the males use their claspers to hold the females and pass sperm into their bodies. The sperm meets and fertilizes the eggs. In some kinds of sharks, a horny case forms around each egg, and the eggs are laid into the water. Eventually they crack open, and a baby shark emerges. In others, the fertilized eggs are kept inside the mother's body until they hatch, so the mother gives birth to baby sharks. Some species produce just a few babies at a time. Others produce batches of 50 or more.

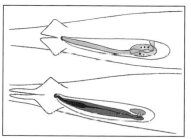

Female (above) and male organs

TEETH

The typical flat, triangular teeth of most sharks grow from the skin of the jaws and are constantly being replaced. They are never fixed in the jaws like those of a reptile or mammal. Some just drop off, but many are probably torn out as the shark feeds. A shark may grow and shed several thousand teeth in its lifetime. Because the teeth are covered with hard, bony material, they last a long time. The seabed all over the world is strewn with discarded shark teeth (see page 19).

GROWING UP

Many sharks start life as eggs, from which baby sharks emerge after several months. Baby sharks look after themselves independently from the moment of hatching or birth. They grow very slowly. Almost every species takes several years to reach maturity and to be able to reproduce. Then they continue growing, even more slowly, probably until they die. How do we know how old they are? Some species add a ring of growth to their vertebrae every year. Others have been tagged and measured in the wild, then caught later and measured again.

Eggs of dogfish and sharks often come in tough, horny cases

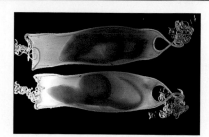

WARM, TEMPERATE AND COLD WATERS

Sharks are found in all the world's oceans, from the warmest to the coldest. They are found, too, at all depths, some living pelagically (entirely at the surface), some in mid-water and many more at different depths on the seabed.

TROPICAL SHARKS

Generally, the biggest, most active sharks are those of surface and mid-waters in the tropics living at temperatures above 68°F (20°C). These include most of the best-known sharks—the ones that live close to the coasts, and most often come into contact with humans. Others, less well known, live in mid-ocean and are seldom seen even from ships. On the seabed below them live other kinds of tropical sharks, usually smaller and more sedentary (stay-at-home), with local rather than worldwide distributions. Many live along the coasts and in deeper waters along the continental shelves.

TEMPERATE-WATER SHARKS

Temperate waters (50–68°F, 10–20°C) have fewer species of sharks, though often the same species occur in both Northern and Southern Hemispheres. They migrate toward the equator as surface waters grow colder in winter, and toward the poles when they warm in summer. Some avoid the warmest surface waters by diving deeper, where the water is always cooler. Again, below them are dozens of temperate seabed species, usually smaller and living more locally.

COLD-WATER SHARKS

A few species of sharks seem to prefer cold water, that is, below 50°F (10°C). They can be found in cool temperate seas of the far north and south, and also in cool layers below the surface waters of warm temperate and subtropical regions. Greenland sharks live successfully in seas that freeze over in winter and remain close to freezing point in summer. On the seabed below them are several bottom-living species, often in enormous shoals that make them worth catching in trawl nets.

AROUND THE WORLD

Where sharks live: how they are spread across the world's oceans in all kinds of waters.

THOUGH TO HUMANS the oceans may seem much the same all over, to fishes and other marine animals they offer many different "habitats," or places to live. The diagram below shows some of the important natural zones or feeding areas where sharks live.

1. COASTAL ZONE

Waters of the shallow area immediately around the coast are often rich in nutrients, which nourish plant life and provide food for fishes and other animals. The seabed may be rocky, or covered with mud (close to river mouths), sand or gravel, which in shallow water support sea grasses and seaweeds.

In deeper water, where plants cannot grow, the seabed supports marine worms, starfish, sea urchins, shellfish and other animals, all of which provide food for fishes. This zone is often rich in bottom-living sharks, and its masses of shoaling fishes attract pelagic sharks too.

2. LAGOON AND REEF ZONE

Tropical coasts are often lined with coral reefs, which provide sandy-bottomed lagoons sheltered from pounding waves, and walls of coral rock that are homes for enormous numbers of small animals. Both the lagoons and the reefs provide food for many hundreds of different kinds of fishes and are favorite haunts for both bottom-living and pelagic sharks.

1. COASTAL ZONE

2. LAGOON AND REEF ZONE

3. SHELF ZONE

3. SHELF ZONE

Around every continent and many islands, at depths down to 330 ft (100 m), the seabed slopes gradually downward to form a submarine "shelf," cut originally by wave action. Beyond this the seabed falls more rapidly to the continental slope and then to the deeper ocean. The shelf, often covered with sand and gravel from the land, and the shallow water above it, provide good feeding areas for shoals of bony fishes and for many different kinds of sharks that feed on them.

Gray nurse shark exploring a coral reef

4. PELAGIC (SURFACE) AND MID-WATER ZONES

Surface and mid-water zones away from the coast are not especially rich in nutrients. Food is often scarce, so the small fish that feed here tend to travel long distances, and the bigger, predatory fish that feed on them must be wanderers too. This is where we find some of the biggest sharks, both the drifting plankton-feeders (whale, basking and megamouth sharks) as well as the big hunters

5. CONTINENTAL SLOPE, DEEP OCEAN BED

Here on the ocean floor, beyond the reach of daylight, there are still plenty of animals, feeding mainly on debris that falls from the richer surface waters above. This zone is beyond the reach of most fishing nets, and we know little of what goes on down there. But bottom-living sharks have been caught on hooks, or seen by underwater cameras, at great depths, even below 10,000 ft (3,000 m).

4. PELAGIC AND MID-WATER ZONES

5. CONTINENTAL SLOPE

Tropical, temperate and cold waters

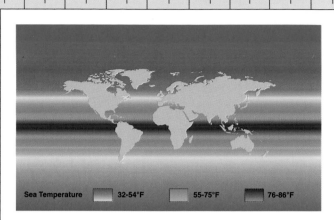

| Sea Temperature | 32-54°F | 55-75°F | 76-86°F |

This map shows the mean annual temperature of surface waters of seas and oceans all over the world. The warmest surface waters, close to the equator, reach more than 82°F (28°C). In the enclosed Red Sea they reach above 86°F (30°C) at the height of summer, falling only a few degrees lower in winter.

Tropical seas are a few degrees warmer in summer than in winter. Temperate seas vary more. Polar seas freeze over in winter and remain at temperatures close to freezing point in winter and summer alike.

THE RICHEST AREAS OF OCEAN

On land there are both deserts, where little or nothing grows, and rich, productive areas full of plants and animals. Much the same is true of the oceans. Tropical oceans far from land are the deserts—the poorest areas where there is little plant life and few animals. You can sail for days in warm, tropical oceans and see very few seabirds, whales or fish, including sharks.

Temperate oceans are richer throughout the year. There are usually plenty of microscopic plants (phytoplankton), tiny animals to feed on them (zooplankton), and fish and seabirds to feed on the animals. Cold oceans are poor in winter, when there is little sunshine, but often very rich in summer. From temperate and cold oceans come most of our commercial fish.

In warm seas or cold, the richest patches are areas close to shore, or among islands where vertical currents bring

water up from the seabed to the surface, or in the open ocean where currents, horizontal or vertical, meet and mix. They are rich because the stirring brings nutrients to the surface. Like fertilizers in a garden, nutrients are chemicals that encourage growth of phytoplankton, which feeds zooplankton, which in turn provides food for the bigger animals. These, then, are the areas where you find the big shoals of fish, seabirds, whales—and often sharks.

White-tip reef sharks in lagoon

OLD SHARKS

Six-gilled, seven-gilled and frilled sharks—called "old" because sharks just like them lived many millions of years ago, and today are found as fossils.

FACT FILE

BLUNT-NOSED SIX-GILLED SHARK

Order:	Hexanchiformes
Family:	Hexanchidae (6- and 7-gilled sharks)
Latin name:	*Hexanchus griseus*
Color:	Gray brown, dark above, paler below
Length:	Up to 15 ft (4.5 m), possibly more
Habitat:	Coastal and shelf waters down to 6,000 ft (1,800 m)
Range:	Wide distribution in cold, temperate and tropical northern seas

BROAD-NOSED SEVEN-GILLED SHARK

Order:	Hexanchiformes
Family:	Hexanchidae (6- and 7-gilled sharks)
Latin name:	*Notorhynchus cepedianus*
Color:	Brown with black spots, paler underneath
Length:	Up to 10 ft (3 m)
Habitat:	Coast, shelf and continental slope to depths approaching 6,500 ft (2,000 m)
Range:	Temperate zones of the South Atlantic, Pacific and Indian Oceans

FRILLED SHARK

Order:	Hexanchiformes
Family:	Chlamydoselachidae (frilled sharks)
Latin name:	*Chlamidoselachus anguineus*
Color:	Brown or gray
Length:	Up to 2 m (6 ft)
Habitat:	Cool coastal and shelf waters, to depths of 4,000 ft (1,200 m)
Range:	Worldwide in cool seas

THE TWO SPECIES OF SIX-GILLED SHARKS live on the edge of the continental shelf in many parts of the northern world, from Iceland in the north to the Mediterranean and Caribbean Seas. They are slim, brown sharks with a single dorsal fin and anal fin set well back, and a long, powerful tail. We know very little about how they live. Deep-sea game fishermen have sometimes hooked them and tried to reel them in, but found them too big and powerful to deal with.

Commercial fishermen used to hunt them for their oil. They have been reported to dive to more than 5,900 ft (1,800 m). They probably feed on other fish near the deep seafloor, but they also take dolphins and swordfish in surface waters.

Broad-nosed seven-gilled shark

Frilled shark

Closely related seven-gilled sharks are usually smaller and more slender, with longer tails. They, too, live on the continental slopes and deep sea-floor, with similar ranges and general habits.

There is just one species of frilled shark, clearly recognizable whether it appears off California, southern Africa or Japan. The six pairs of gill clefts on either side, with leading edges frilled like piecrusts, identify it straight away. Another unusual feature is the big mouth, with wide jaws right at the front of the body, and sharp, spiny, hooked teeth. The eyes and nostrils are unusually large.

These are long, slender, streamlined sharks, flexible like eels. The single dorsal and anal fins probably act like additional tail flukes, helping to push the fish forward into crevices and between rocks. Frilled sharks live in deep water, which even in the tropics, tends to be cold. The first few specimens were reported more than 100 years ago from the North Pacific Ocean. Now frilled sharks have been caught in deep waters off Madeira, Norway, Africa, California, Australia and New Zealand. They breed by "ovovivipary"—that is, by producing 8 to 12 eggs that stay inside the body until they have hatched. We know very little else about their behavior or biology.

FIVE, SIX OR SEVEN GILLS?

Why do some sharks have six pairs of gill and some seven, while most have only five? We do not know. Many millions of years ago the ancestors of all the vertebrates probably had a dozen or more pairs of gill slits. The first two pairs were modified to form the upper and lower jaws. By the time fish had evolved, the number was reduced to five, six or seven, and most bony and cartilaginous fish settled for five. Sharks and rays in fact have an extra small slit—called the "spiracle"—which in some serves as an extra tiny gill.

Gills provide a big surface, well supplied with blood, that takes oxygen from the water as it flows past. In the course of evolution, when vertebrates first began to leave the sea and inhabit the land, gills were replaced by lungs, which are much more efficient for breathing air. However, reptiles, birds and mammals—even humans—still have tiny gills for a short time when they are developing as embryos, in the egg or the uterus.

Where do we find them?

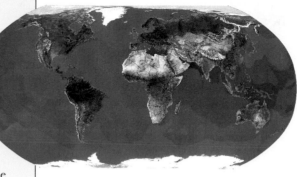

We find old sharks mainly in shelf areas of the Northern Hemisphere, but they also live in deeper waters and may be worldwide

HISTORY OF SHARKS

Cartilage is much softer than bone and tends to break down when a shark dies. So bodies of sharks that died and sank to the seabed have not left very good fossils, except occasionally as imprints that showed their overall size and shape. However, shark teeth and denticles are very hard indeed and have left a good record going back hundreds of millions of years.

The earliest sharks that were recognizable ancestors of modern sharks, skates and rays probably lived more than 350 million years ago. By about 150 million years ago, there were sharks very similar to some of our modern ones—swift, slender hunters with sharp, serrated teeth. Many of the species that we know as fossils later died out. Other kinds lived on, developing into the orders and families we know today.

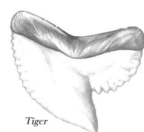
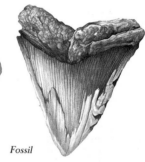

Blue   *Tiger*   *Fossil*

RELATIONSHIPS

These three species represent the two families of the most primitive order of sharks, the Hexanchiformes. "Primitive" does not mean inefficient. It means that biologists think they may be like the early ancestors of all sharks. Primitive features include (a) the comblike lower teeth of the six-gilled and seven-gilled sharks (similar to teeth found in fossil deposits almost 200 million years old), (b) the loose jaw structure, (c) the soft, boneless vertebrae and (d) the extra gills, which in more specialized modern sharks are reduced to five per side.

There are two kinds of six-gilled sharks, two kinds of seven-gilled and just one kind of frilled shark.

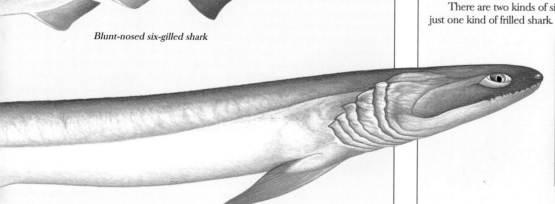

Blunt-nosed six-gilled shark

Broad-nosed seven-gilled shark

FACT FILE
SPINY DOGFISH SHARK

Order:	Squaliformes
Family:	Squalidae (dogfish sharks)
Latin name:	*Squalus acanthias*
Color:	Slate gray to brown, with white spots
Length:	Up to 5 ft (1.5 m)
Habitat:	Cold bottom waters of shelf and continental slopes
Range:	Temperate and cool Pacific and Atlantic Oceans, Mediterranean and Black Seas

GREENLAND SHARK

Order:	Squaliformes
Family:	Squalidae (dogfish sharks)
Latin name:	*Somniosus microcephalus*
Color:	Various: pink, brown, purple gray
Length:	Up to 21 ft (6.5 m)
Habitat:	Shallow shelf waters, and cold, deep waters to 2,000 ft (600 m)
Range:	Greenland and North Atlantic Ocean

BRAMBLE SHARK

Order:	Squaliformes
Family:	Echinorhinidae (bramble sharks)
Latin name:	*Echinorhinus brucus*
Color:	Gray brown spotted back, paler underneath
Length:	Up to 10 ft (3 m)
Habitat:	Cold shelf and continental slope waters
Range:	Coasts and slopes of western Europe and Africa, and Mediterranean Sea

PRICKLY DOGFISH SHARK

Order:	Squaliformes
Family:	Oxynotidae (rough sharks)
Latin name:	*Oxynotus bruniensis*
Color:	Gray brown
Length:	Up to 2.5 ft (75 cm)
Habitat:	Temperate waters of shelf and continental slopes
Range:	Australia, New Zealand, southwest Pacific Ocean

DOGFISH SHARKS

Dogfish sharks, bramble, Greenland and rough sharks: small and great sharks of continental shelf and slopes. Do not confuse them with "dogfish" (page 35).

DOGFISH SHARKS ALL HAVE TWO DORSAL FINS but no anal fin. Typically they are long and slender, around 3.3 ft (1 m) long. There are about 70 species, here represented by the spiny dogfish. However, one group called the "sleeper sharks," including the Greenland shark shown here, grow much bigger. Dogfish sharks feed mainly on the seabed, but also come up into shallow water.

Spiny dogfish are so-called because of a sharp, pointed spine on the leading edge of each dorsal fin. They come up in the thousands into shallow water in spring, and again in autumn. Between seasons they disappear into the depths. Commercial fishermen know when to expect them and catch many thousands of tons each year for meat and oil.

The sleeper sharks grow much larger and live in some of the coldest seas. Why sleeper sharks? Probably because, when caught and hauled up from very cold water, they tend to be sluggish and inactive. The Greenland shark, one of the biggest, grows up to 21 ft (6.5 m) long. Sleeper sharks are common off the cold coasts of the northern Atlantic Ocean. Through the 1800s and early 1900s many thousands were taken for oil and meat off Iceland, Greenland and northern Norway. Fishermen still catch them there by harpoon and hook. They appear, too, in warmer waters, attracted to fish canneries and other places where meaty offal is thrown into the sea. Bramble sharks are fatter than true dogfish sharks, with their two dorsal fins set far back toward the tail. Their name comes from the thorns, just like those of a bramble or rose bush, up to 0.5 in (12 mm) long, scattered over their surface.

Prickly dogfish shark

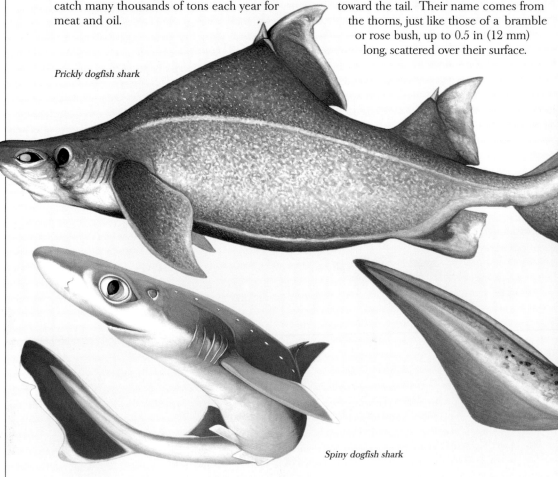

Spiny dogfish shark

They are not common but are caught occasionally on lines or in deep-water fishing nets in the Mediterranean Sea and off West Africa. Fishermen who try to handle them without gloves get badly scratched, and the thorns carry bacteria, which may poison the scratches. A similar and closely related species called the prickly shark (*Echinorhinus cookei*), also covered with sharp thorns, lives in deep lagoons and open seas off islands in the Pacific Ocean.

THE SMALLEST SHARKS

Smallest of all the sharks are the tiny-spined pygmy sharks, *Squaliolus laticaudus,* about 6 in (15 cm) long when fully grown. They live in surface waters of the tropical Pacific Ocean.

Here is a dwarf shark 12–15 in (30–38 cm) long

ROUGH SHARKS

Prickly dogfish are one of the five species of rough sharks, so-called from their rough skin. These are small sharks with bodies flattened from side to side and ridges along their back and abdomen. The tall dorsal fins give rough sharks their strange, angular appearance. They are quite common in deep water off New Zealand and Australia. The mouth is small with fleshy lips and small teeth. We know little of how rough sharks live, but they probably browse on the seabed, sucking up invertebrate animals such as worms, sea slugs and shellfish.

BREEDING

Dogfish sharks are ovoviviparous (o-vo-vi-**vip**-a-rus). This means that the females produce eggs that are fertilized internally, but the eggs are never laid. Instead they hatch inside the mother's body, and after several months the fully formed pups are born. Spiny dogfish and bramble sharks produce 20 to 30 young at a time, each up to 1 ft (30 cm) long. Rough sharks produce 6 or 7, each about 4 in (10 cm) long. The young fish probably follow their mother for a short time, feeding where she feeds, but we know little of this part of their life.

Where do we find them?

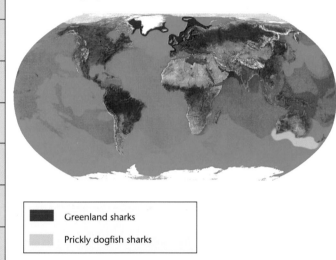

Spiny dogfish and other very similar "true" dogfish sharks live in coastal and shelf waters all over the world. Greenland sharks live in deeper waters around the northern Atlantic Ocean, often coming up to the surface as well. Bramble sharks are caught mainly off western Europe and West Africa, and in the Mediterranean Sea. Prickly dogfish are found on the seabed around Australia and New Zealand.

■ Greenland sharks

■ Prickly dogfish sharks

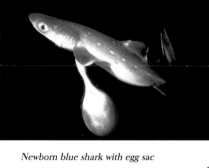

Newborn blue shark with egg sac

RELATIONSHIPS

Sailors fishing over the side of their ship in clear waters often saw groups of small, dark sharks, hunting in packs like dogs. They called them "dogfish," and the name is still given to many different kinds of small, bottom-feeding sharks. The "dogfish sharks," grouped together in the order Squaliformes, are mostly of this habit. All have two dorsal fins but no anal fin. Confusingly, many other kinds of small sharks, belonging to other orders and with anal fins, also have "dogfish" in their name. So we take care always to give "dogfish sharks" their full name.

The biggest family is the Squalidae, with more than 70 species. We call these the typical or "true" dogfish sharks. Most grow to about 5 ft (1.5 m), but Greenland sharks can be four times as long and the smallest, spined pygmy sharks, are less than 6 in (15 cm) long. The two kinds of bramble sharks are quite different, and so are the five kinds of rough sharks, so these go into separate families.

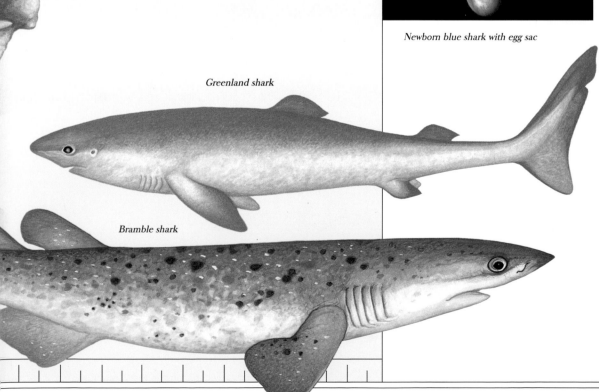

Greenland shark

Bramble shark

SAW SHARKS

*Sharks of tropical waters that carry a two-edged saw,
set with hard spiny teeth, on their nose.*

THERE ARE SEVERAL FORMS of sharks that though basically similar to the "typical" shark shown on pages 8–9, have developed some special features that immediately set them apart from the rest. The saw sharks, or Pristiophoriformes, are a good example. "Pristio" is based on the Greek word for saw. Their scientific name Pristiophorus, from which come their order and family names, means "saw-carrier."

In body, with their two tall, triangular dorsal fins, slender, powerful tail and lack of anal fins, the saw sharks are not unlike some of the dogfish sharks. However, their front end is quite different. It is as though their upper jaw has been pulled out to form a long point, and a row of sharp, uneven spiny teeth has been set along either edge. The head and front of the body are slightly flattened, with the eyes and spiracles set in grooves on top. There is a small mouth underneath, lined with two or three rows of small, single-pointed teeth for grabbing and holding prey.

Scuba divers often see saw sharks lying close to the seabed, resting on sandy or muddy surfaces. They are quite harmless unless you touch one or stand on it accidentally. In trying to escape or wriggle free, it may cut you quite deeply with its saw. When undisturbed, saw sharks swim slowly, flicking the long tail and using the big pectoral fins to adjust their height above the bottom.

Resting saw sharks dig themselves slightly into the surface, letting sand or mud settle on them so that they merge with their background. In this position they cannot use their mouth (which is underneath the head) to draw in water for breathing. Instead they draw water inwards through the large spiracle above the eyes, and pass it out through the gills.

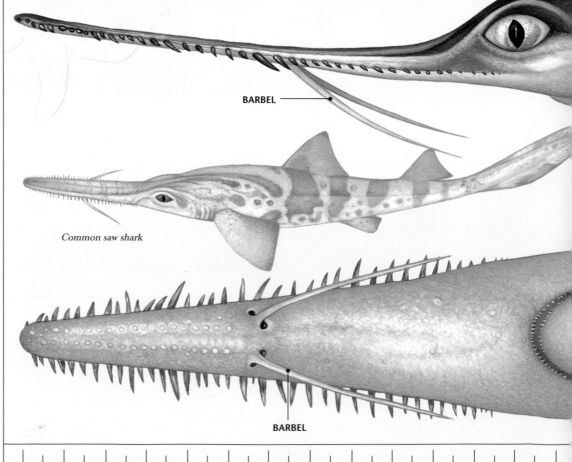

BARBEL

Common saw shark

BARBEL

Where do we find them?

FEEDING

For hunting, saw sharks have two "barbels," or strands, hanging from the saw, one on either side, which are sensitive to taste or scent. When the shark swims slowly over the bottom, the barbels trail, picking up chemical messages from the seabed. They detect the presence of food, small shrimps, worms or shellfish that the shark cannot see.

On finding prey, the shark dips its flat snout into the seabed, wriggles it to stir up the sand or mud, and grabs and swallows the food that floats out.

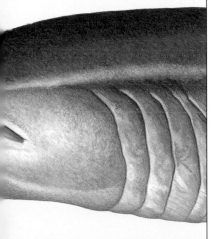

Side view (above) and underside (below) of short-nosed saw shark. The long barbels are organs of touch

BREEDING

Saw sharks, like dogfish sharks, are ovoviviparous. Because the embryos take more than a year to develop from eggs, females are believed to breed every second year. The saw remains soft and folded away while the embryos are growing, straightening and hardening after birth. Up to 20 young are born at a time.

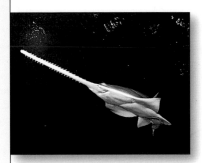

Saw shark

SAWFISHES

Among the rays (pages 40–41), which are closely related to sharks, there is one family that, like the saw sharks, carries two edged saws. These are the sawfish (family Pristidae). There are several species, and all live in warm, shallow tropical seas, estuaries or rivers. Like other rays, they tend to be kite-shaped, with pectoral fins joined to the head, and their gills are on the underside of the body, not on top. Fully grown sawfish are much larger than saw sharks, up to 21 ft (6.5 m) long. Simply because they are so big, with very sharp sawteeth, they can be very dangerous if you tread on them or catch one on a line.

Open mouth and saw of common saw shark

Fossils show that saw sharks have existed for more than 70 million years and may formerly have been more widespread and plentiful than they are today. However, common and short-nosed saw sharks are well known in shallow coastal waters of south-eastern, southern and southwestern Australia, down to about 300 ft (90 m). Elsewhere, common saw sharks are found in similar coastal waters from the Philippine Islands to Korea, and a similar species, the Japanese saw shark, *Pristiophorus japonicus*, lives off Japan. In parts of their range, saw sharks are plentiful enough to be caught commercially for oil and meat. A similar five-gilled species lives in shallow waters of the Caribbean Sea, and a six-gilled species, *Pliotrema warreni*, lives off the southern coasts of South Africa.

Saw sharks

Common saw shark with barbels trailing, "sniffing" the ground below the sand

RELATIONSHIPS

The saw sharks form a small order of about five species, all in a single family, but living in different parts of the world. Like the dogfish sharks (pages 20–21), they have two dorsal fins but no anal fin. This may mean that the two orders are closely related. Most of them have five gill slits on either side, though one species has six. But all saw sharks have a single feature that sets them apart—their long, narrow snout, with rows of flat, spiny teeth on either side. No other kind of shark has a nose like this, though rather similar saws are carried by some of the rays (see pages 40–41) and even by bony fishes.

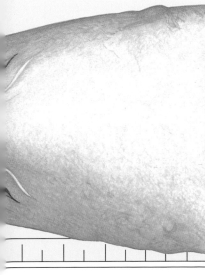

ANGELS AND BULLHEADS

Angels, bullheads and Port Jackson sharks of sandy and muddy seabeds.

FACT FILE
CALIFORNIAN BULLHEAD SHARK

Order:	Heterodontiformes
Family:	Heterodontidae (bullhead sharks)
Latin name:	*Heterodontus francisci*
Color:	Buff mottled with pale brown, dark brown spots
Length:	Up to 3.3 ft (1 m)
Habitat:	Sandy seabeds in warm shallow water down to 1,000 ft (300 m)
Range:	Central to southern California coast

PACIFIC ANGEL SHARK

Order:	Squatiniformes
Family:	Squatinidae (angel sharks)
Latin name:	*Squatina californica*
Color:	Fawn or gray brown with dark brown spots
Length:	Up to 5 ft (1.5 m)
Habitat:	Sandy seabeds down to 330 ft (100 m), occasionally deeper
Range:	Coastal and continental slopes of the temperate and tropical eastern Pacific Ocean

PORT JACKSON SHARK

Order:	Heterodontiformes
Family:	Heterodontidae (bullhead sharks)
Latin name:	*Heterodontus portusjacksoni*
Color:	Greenish fawn mottled with dark brown bars and stripes
Length:	Up to 5 ft (1.5 m)
Habitat:	Sandy or rocky sea-beds, in warm shallow water down to 1,000 ft (300 m)
Range:	Subtropical and temperate shores of Australia and New Zealand

Angel SHARKS AT FIRST GLANCE look very much like some of the bottom-living skates and rays (pages 40–41)—flattened, kite-shaped, with broad pelvic and pectoral fins, small dorsal fins and short but powerful stubby tails. However, they are true sharks. Unlike rays, the head is separated by deep grooves from the pectoral fins, and the gill slits are on the lower flanks of the body, rather than underneath. As the fossil record shows, sharks with this form first appeared in shallow, muddy seas more than 200 million years ago.

Port Jackson shark

They live in warm, shallow coastal seas all over the world. The species shown here lives along the eastern shore of the North Pacific Ocean. There is a very similar species (some say the same) along the coast of Chile, and other kinds live off western Europe, northwestern and western Africa, the Indian Ocean shores of southeastern Africa, southern Australia, Korea and Japan. Wherever found, they dig themselves into the sand during the day, then become active at night, lying low and snapping at passing fish. They are easily caught in trawl nets or with baited hooks, and many people find them good to eat.

Like frilled and six-gilled sharks, bullhead sharks have a very long fossil record, first appearing as long as 160 million years ago.

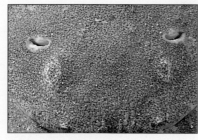

The rough skin of an angel shark, protected by tiny toothlike scales

With broad, square heads, a ridge over each cowlike eye, the mouth well forward and broad pectoral fins, they are small but powerful-looking sharks. The two dorsal fins are tall and triangular, with a sharp, horn-like spike in front of each that gives them the alternative name of "horn sharks." Californian bullhead sharks live in temperate and warm coastal waters off central and southern California. Other species are found in similar habitats of Japan, Ecuador, southern Africa and Australia.

Port Jackson sharks bear the original name for the harbor of Sydney, Australia, where they were first discovered. Port Jackson sharks have all the main features of bullheads, with an even more powerful, boxlike body. They, too, live on the seabed, often among rocks and caverns where they hunt for mussels, clams and other shellfish. Divers report that they often lie up during the day, becoming more active and moving around during evenings and at night.

Pacific angel shark

DIFFERENT TEETH

Their Greek name Heterodontus, meaning "different teeth," refers to the different kinds of teeth that are found in the mouths of heterodont sharks. Those at the edges of the mouth are sharp and grasping, but the ones in the middle of each row are flat and platelike.

Nostrils and teeth of Port Jackson shark

These sharks eat fish and a range of invertebrates, such as worms and crabs, but their very powerful jaws and teeth are specialized for crushing hard foods, probably mussels, small clams, oysters, limpets and other shellfish. The sharp teeth probably grasp and turn the prey; the flat teeth break the shells like nutcrackers.

Californian bullhead shark

HOW ANGEL SHARKS LIVE

By marking California angel sharks with electronic tags and plotting their movements, scientists have shown that these sharks spend much of their day half buried in the sea floor. They become active in the evenings, hunting over a few hundred square yards of seafloor, then often returning to the same base as before to digest their meals. Some travel up to 5 miles (9 km) a night. In winter, many drop away into deeper water, returning to the shallows and taking up their feeding territories in spring.

Where do we find them?

Pacific angel sharks live in shallow water along the Californian coast. Other species of angel sharks occur in similar habitats along other warm-temperate coasts. Californian bullhead sharks, too, live along the California coast, while the rest of the bullheads are found in the Pacific and Indian Oceans. Port Jackson sharks are limited to cooler waters of Australia and New Zealand.

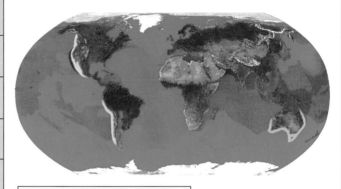

- ■ Californian bullhead sharks
- □ Pacific angel sharks
- ▨ Port Jackson sharks

BREEDING

Angel sharks are ovoviviparous, producing eggs that they keep inside them, and giving birth when the pups reach the right size. Pacific angel sharks produce up to 13 pups each litter, and probably breed every second or third year.

Bullhead sharks, including Port Jackson sharks, are oviparous, covering their fertile eggs in horny casings and laying between 6 and 10 over a period of two or three months. Eggs of these species have a stiff, spiral-shaped shell, pointed at one end. Several mother sharks may lay their eggs together in "nursery" areas, hiding them away deep among the rocks so that predators cannot gobble them up. That is all the care they give them. The eggs take between six months and a year to develop and hatch. The young sharks continue to grow very slowly after hatching, reaching breeding size when they are about 10 years old.

RELATIONSHIPS

These squat, flattened fishes represent two small orders of sharks, quite different from all other kinds. About a dozen species of angel sharks, all very similar in appearance and included in a single family, are widely distributed around the world in cool temperate and tropical waters. Bullhead sharks form an even smaller group, with only about eight species, again in a single family. They are found only in the warm Indian and Pacific Oceans. All the angel sharks and bullhead sharks are adapted for feeding on the seabed.

FACT FILE
NURSE SHARK

Order:	Orectolobiformes
Family:	Ginglymostomatidae (nurse sharks)
Latin name:	*Ginglymostoma cirratum*
Color:	Brown or gray, usually plain, dark above, paler below
Length:	Up to 13 ft (4 m)
Habitat:	Shallow coastal seas
Range:	Warm waters off northern Australia and Papua New Guinea

NECKLACE CARPET SHARK

Order:	Orectolobiformes
Family:	Parascyllidae (collared carpet sharks)
Latin name:	*Parascyllium collare*
Color:	Dark brown to black, with patterns of white spots on back, paler underneath
Length:	Up to 3.3 ft (1 m)
Habitat:	Shallow rock reefs and sandy beaches
Range:	Southern coast of Australia

ORNATE WOBBEGONG

Order:	Orectolobiformes
Family:	Orectolobidae (wobbegongs)
Latin name:	*Orectolobus ornatus*
Color:	Brown blotched with gray and tan, varying to match seabed backgrounds
Length:	Up to 11.5 ft (3.5 m)
Habitat:	Coral reefs and sandy seabed down to 390 ft (120 m)
Range:	Warm waters off northern Australia and Papua New Guinea

Nurse shark nosing among marine algae and corals

CARPET SHARKS, WOBBEGONGS & NURSES

Colorful sharks of the seabed in the warm shallow waters of the world.

THE ORECTOLOBE (O-**RECT**-TOE-LOBE) SHARKS are small to medium sized, often brightly colored to match backgrounds of reefs, seaweed, gravel and sand. All live in warm shallow water, usually close to coral reefs or sandy lagoons. Many are flattened, so they sit more comfortably on the seabed. All have complex lips with sensory barbels and lobes, suggesting that they hunt mainly by touch, taste and smell.

Carpet sharks take their name from their bright colors and patterns. Most are slender and eel-like. Of the two families, collared carpet sharks are long and slim, with a dark band around the head. Long-tailed carpet sharks are even longer and slimmer, with thin but powerful tails. Necklace sharks are among the most beautiful of the collared carpet sharks, with jewel-like patterns along their flanks.

By contrast the six species of wobbegongs are broad and flat, with huge heads and wing-like pectoral fins, almost like those of angel sharks (pages 24–25). Some are brightly colored with patterns of green, tan and gold. Others, like this ornate wobbegong, are decorated not only with patches of color, but with tassels and barbels that help to break up their outline and make them almost invisible. Many Australian scuba divers have stood on what they thought was a patch of rocky sea floor and found it to be a 10-foot-long wobbegong. Fortunately for them, wobbegongs are not man-eaters. If disturbed, they usually disappear in a cloud of sand. Their food is mainly small fish and invertebrate animals of the seafloor.

Nurse sharks are the largest and most lively of the group. Though quiet and sleepy during the day, they become more active after sundown, when they swim slowly over the reefs in search of prey. Some grow very large, but they are neither fierce nor dangerous to man.

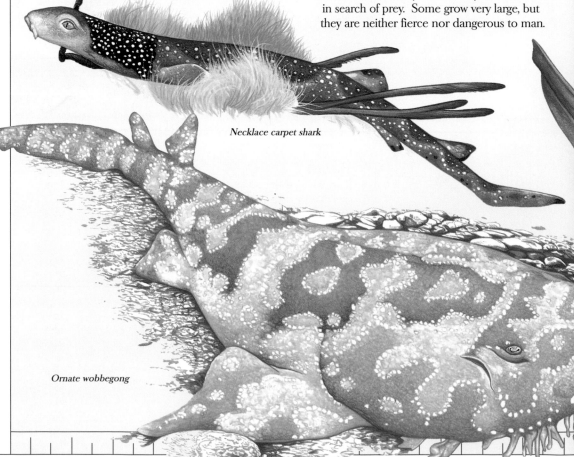

Necklace carpet shark

Ornate wobbegong

Where do we find them?

Like other sharks in this order, they feed mainly by browsing and sucking food from the seafloor, rather than chasing active prey. Their mouths are soft. They lack the gaping jaws and rows of sharp teeth of the man-eaters.

Divers who give them plenty of space have nothing to fear from nurse sharks. Sadly, nurse sharks have much to fear from humans. Because they are big, and sometimes inquisitive, they are often mistaken for man-eaters and killed quite unnecessarily.

Spotted wobbegong matching its spotted background

BREEDING

Necklace carpet sharks lay eggs with horny shells, which they anchor with tendrils to strands of seaweed and coral. Wobbegongs and nurse sharks give birth to live young, about a dozen at a time.

SELF-PROTECTION

We think of sharks and rays mainly as predators—that is, animals that hunt and kill other animals. But they are also prey—animals that are killed by others. The smaller species are particularly at risk from larger ones. How do they protect themselves against attack?

- Being dark-colored on top and pale underneath makes them harder to see from above or below.
- Those that live on or near the bottom may be colored to look like the seabed, or shaped to look like weed-covered rocks.
- Moving about in shoals (big groups) reduces the chances of any one being caught.
- Spines, thorns, poison glands and electric shocks hurt or damage any predator (including fishermen) that tries to catch them.

Look out for these different forms of self-protection in the sharks described in this book.

Necklace carpet sharks are restricted almost entirely to the southern coasts of Australia. Other collared carpet sharks occur more widely in Australian waters, others again off the Philippine Islands, and along the coasts of China and Japan. Wobbegongs are mainly Australian (their name was given to them by Australian aboriginals), and the ornate wobbegong is restricted to Australia and neighboring Papua New Guinea. But other species occur off Japan and the northwestern Pacific Ocean. Nurse sharks range more widely. This species lives along the tropical Pacific Ocean coasts of Mexico and Peru, along the western Atlantic Ocean coast from New England to Brazil and off the tropical west coast of Africa.

■	Carpet sharks and wobbegongs
▨	Nurse sharks

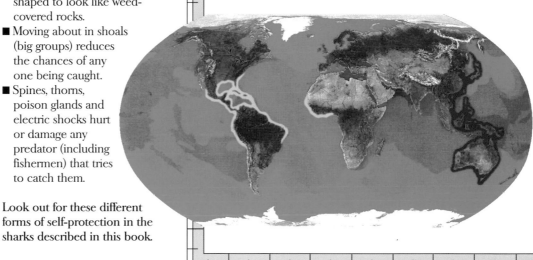

WHY NURSE SHARKS?

How did nurse sharks get their name? Nobody knows for sure. Some say it is because they are plain gray or brown, like nurses in uniform. Others say it is because they suck their food from the seabed with a noise like that of a nursing (suckling) calf or foal. Their scientific name, *Ginglymostoma*, means "flexible mouth," perhaps because of the soft lips that form a suction cup when they are feeding.

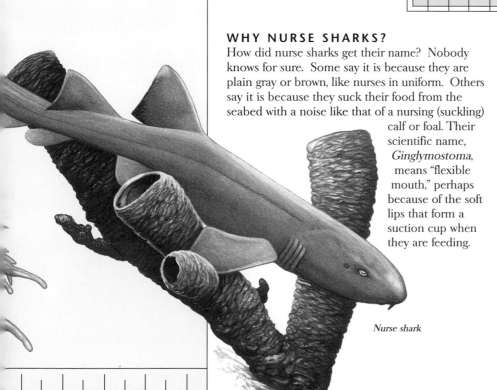

Nurse shark

RELATIONSHIPS

This is an order of about 33 species of sharks, divided into seven families. All have two dorsal fins and an anal fin. The fins have no protective spines. In all these sharks, the mouth is well forward, and the lips are complicated by lobes, grooves and barbels.

They are mostly warm-water sharks, living especially in and around coral reefs and lagoons. Many of them are brightly colored and decorated with barbels that help them to match their backgrounds. Two of the familes, the zebra sharks and whale sharks, have one species each. The blind sharks (which are not blind, but look as though they might be) have two species, the nurse sharks three, and the wobbegongs six. The largest families are those of the collared carpet sharks with seven species, and the long-tailed carpet sharks with 13. Here and on the next pages we illustrate four of the families.

FACT FILE
WHALE SHARK

Order:	Orectolobiformes
Family:	Rhiniodontidae (whale sharks)
Latin name:	*Rhiniodon typus*
Color:	Blue gray with patterns of paler spots on back, paler gray underneath
Length:	Up to 50 ft (15 m)
Habitat:	Warm surface waters, usually oceanic and far from land
Range:	Offshore waters of all warm temperate and tropical oceans

BASKING SHARK

Order:	Lamniformes
Family:	Cetorhinidae (basking sharks)
Latin name:	*Cetorhinus maximus*
Color:	Dark blue gray on top, paler underneath
Length:	Up to 28 ft (12 m)
Habitat:	Cool surface waters, mostly close to shore
Range:	Coastal zones of all cool temperate oceans, north and south

MEGAMOUTH SHARK

Order:	Lamniformes
Family:	Megachasmidae (megamouth shark)
Latin name:	*Megachasma pelagios*
Color:	Dark brown on top, paler underneath
Length:	Up to 15 ft (4.5 m)
Habitat:	Cool offshore waters, below 330 ft (100 m)
Range:	Central and eastern Pacific Ocean

Whale shark

WHALE SHARKS, BASKING SHARKS

Gigantic but gentle: whale sharks, basking sharks, and megamouths.

MOST PEOPLE SEEING A WHALE SHARK or basking shark for the first time simply cannot believe their eyes. Is it an island? A rock? A huge tree trunk? The bottom of an overturned ship? Not until you see them moving slightly do you realize that they are alive. When you make out the big dorsal fins, the tiny eyes, the gill clefts and the twitching tail lobe, you realize that you are seeing one of the oceans' two most impressive species of sharks.

How do you tell whale sharks from basking sharks? At first they look rather similar, but in the ocean there is no mistaking them. For a start, they live in quite different waters, with little overlap.

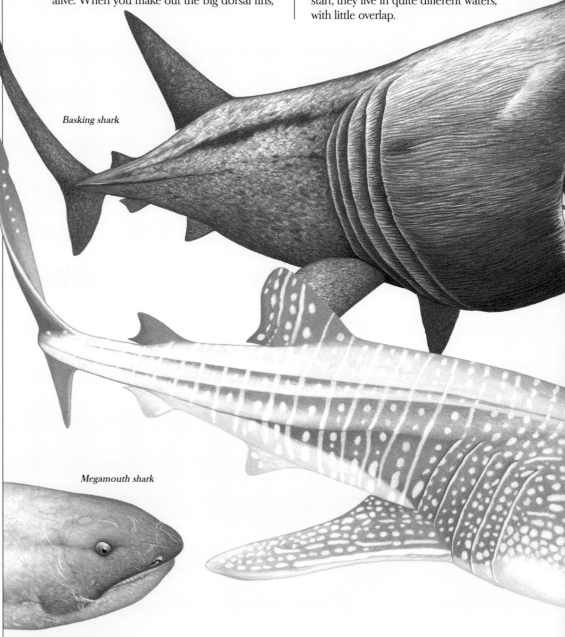

Basking shark

Megamouth shark

Then look at them more closely, and you see all kinds of differences. Whale sharks are flatter and more table-like, with a blunt, flattened head. Basking sharks are rounder, like fat torpedoes, with a tapering, pointed head. Whale sharks have five gill slits like narrow cuts on either side, just before the pectoral fins. Basking sharks have five huge gill openings, which seem to circle the neck like overlapping collars.

Whale sharks have distinctive patterns of pale spots in rows and swirls. Basking sharks are much plainer. This difference does not always show in the water, because sunlight shining through the surface gives both of them a dappled pattern.

Both species feed by swimming slowly into shoals of plankton or small fish, taking huge gulps of seawater. The water passes out through the gill slits. The food is held back by strainers and is pressed down the throat by the huge tongue. For much of the time, both these sharks seem just to drift with the currents. When feeding, they push themselves forward with occasional sweeps of the tail. Neither species is especially plentiful, and both drop quietly down to depths of a few yards if disturbed. Observers on fast-moving ships seldom see them. Yachtsmen more often report them, perhaps because yachts are quieter and can get closer without disturbing them.

VISITING BASKING SHARKS

Coastal fishermen who used to hunt basking sharks for their oil and meat now find it more profitable to take parties out to see them. Basking sharks move seasonally, away from the equator in summer and toward it in winter. Fishermen who know the local currents and movements of fish shoals can usually tell when the basking sharks will arrive, and where they are likely to be found from day to day.

Basking sharks are completely harmless and very tolerant of disturbance. Swimmers and divers can play in the water around them. But they are very big and strong, and a flick of their tail could damage a boat severely. So sensible shark watchers keep at least a shark's-length away from them.

Basking shark

MEGAMOUTHS

Very few people have had the chance to see a megamouth shark. The first was caught in 1976 off Hawaii, and only about a dozen have appeared since. They live in the warm eastern Pacific Ocean, in mid-water over the continental slope. Through the huge mouth (that is what their name means) they draw in water and plankton, which they filter through a network of spines growing from the gills—much like basking sharks.

Megamouth sharks are a reminder that there are probably many more species of sharks, still undiscovered, in mid-waters and deep waters of the oceans.

Whale shark

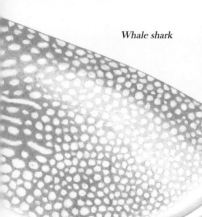

Where do we find them?

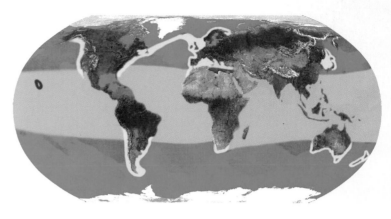

Whale sharks and basking sharks live in different parts of the oceans, with only slight overlap.

If you meet a huge, peaceful shark, lying at the surface in warm tropical or subtropical waters, well out of sight of land, it is almost certainly a whale shark. They are found in tropical waters far out in all three oceans, lying close to the surface, sometimes with dorsal fin and upper tail lobe showing.

If you meet a big shark in cold, cool or temperate waters, in a narrow sea (like the North Sea or Irish Channel, with land on either side), between coastal islands or close to land, it is more likely to be a basking shark. These come close to land in many places where they are easy to see. Like whale sharks, they drift at the surface, swimming very slowly forward while feeding, dropping a few yards if disturbed. Their movements are more purposeful than they seem. They hunt in areas of opposing currents, where the plankton is most plentiful.

Megamouth sharks have been found only off Hawaii, Japan and neighboring coasts. They live mainly in deep water during the day, rising toward the surface at night.

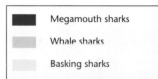

■	Megamouth sharks
	Whale sharks
	Basking sharks

RELATIONSHIPS

Though similar in their enormous size and way of life, whale sharks and basking sharks are only distantly related. Whale sharks belong to the carpet shark group (Orectolobiformes, pages 26–27), most of which live on the seabed. Basking sharks belong to the mackerel shark group (Lamniformes, pages 30–33), which includes both seabed and surface-living forms. Megamouth sharks, first reported in 1976, are also grouped with the mackerel sharks, though we know very little about them. Fewer than a dozen specimens have been caught and examined. They seem to be close relations of basking sharks. Like them, they feed by filtering rather than active hunting.

Whale shark with mouth wide open for feeding

FACT FILE
PORBEAGLE SHARK

Order:	Lamniformes
Family:	Alopiidae (thresher sharks)
Latin name:	*Lamna nasus*
Color:	Dark blue gray above, pale gray to white below
Length:	Up to 11.5 ft (3.5 m)
Habitat:	Coastal, island and continental shelf waters down to 1,300 ft (400 m)
Range:	Temperate and cool coasts of the North Atlantic, South Atlantic and South Pacific Oceans

COMMON THRESHER SHARK

Order:	Lamniformes
Family:	Alopiidae (thresher sharks)
Latin name:	*Alopias vulpinus*
Color:	Dark blue gray above, white below
Length:	Up to 20 ft (6 m)
Habitat:	Coastal, island and continental-shelf waters down to 1,300 ft (400 m)
Range:	Tropical, temperate and cool areas of the Atlantic Ocean, and the central and west Pacific Ocean

SHORT-FINNED MAKO SHARK

Order:	Lamniformes
Family:	Lamnidae
Latin name:	*Isurus oxyrinchus*
Color:	Dark blue on top, white underneath
Length:	Up to 13 ft (4 m)
Habitat:	Offshore surface waters down to 500 ft (150 m)
Range:	Worldwide in tropical and temperate oceans

MACKEREL SHARKS

1. Porbeagles, threshers and makos: monster mackerel sharks of surface waters in most of the world's oceans.

WE HEAR A LOT about fierce, man-eating sharks in tropical or subtropical waters. But there are sharks big enough to be man-eaters in cooler waters too. Porbeagles and common thresher sharks are some of the big sharks you might see on a fishing trip off the coast of Britain, Germany, New England, Canada, or a dozen other places where the climate is temperate and the water cool. The name "porbeagle" comes from Cornwall, in southwest England, where these sharks are often seen.

Porbeagles are tubby, streamlined blue sharks, with pointed faces and large eyes. They have big, sail-like front dorsal fins and much smaller rear dorsal fins close to the tail. The tails are large, with lobes almost equal, and sharp ridges on either side of the base. The gill slits are wide, and the mouth, lined with fine pointed teeth, lies well back under the nose. If you see one, you usually see several together, darting like dolphins through shoals of fish close to the surface. They feed mainly on small fish in surface and mid-water shoals, but also take larger fish, squid and probably shellfish from the continental shelf and slopes.

Common thresher sharks are often seen with porbeagles, feeding close inshore on the same shoals of small fish. You know them immediately by the huge, long upper lobe of the tail. Their pectoral and pelvic fins, too, are much longer than those of porbeagles. These are very lively sharks. They beat the water with their tails (probably to scare the fish into small, tight bunches) and often leap clear of the surface like breaching whales.

Common thresher

Porbeagle tail

RIDGES

Mako sharks are more slender than porbeagles, with smaller fins and bigger, more rugged teeth. They probably move faster and take larger prey than porbeagles, and range more widely across the warmer oceans of the world. Short-finned makos appear in all oceans. Long-finned makos, which are closely related and very similar, occur only in the Pacific Ocean.

Wherever they are found, makos have a reputation for ferocity. They eat many small shoaling fish, but also attack swordfish, tuna and other fast-moving surface fish. Sport fishermen love to hook them, because they fight hard when caught, swimming fast, leaping into the air and giving up only after several hours when they are completely exhausted. They have been known to attack boats (particularly white ones) and eat people when they find them in the water.

WARM-BLOODED

Many of the big mackerel sharks, including porbeagles, makos and great white sharks, are unusual among fish in being warm-blooded. Heat generated in muscles while they are swimming recirculates through the body, keeping their overall temperature up to 20°F (11°C) higher than that of the

Mako shark

water surrounding them. This allows them to travel faster, and possibly to twist and turn more quickly, making them more efficient. But it costs them more in food and oxygen. They have to hunt more than sleepier, less active kinds of sharks, and they have to keep moving all the time to take in enough oxygen through their gills.

BREEDING

Lke many other kinds of shark, porbeagle, thresher and mako sharks are ovoviviparous, though with a difference from some other kinds.

Females produce several dozen small eggs that collect together in the oviducts, some fertile, others not. Only the fertile eggs start to develop. The embryos live on the yolk of their own eggs until they are about 2.7 in (7 cm) long, then start to feed on the smaller embryos and infertile eggs around them. The result—just a few large pups, usually between three and a dozen, are born at a time.

Where do we find them?

Porbeagles are found in waters of the North Atlantic Ocean. Very similar sharks that some biologists think are the same species (others think they are very closely related) occur off temperate shores of Australia, New Zealand and South America. Another close relative, the salmon shark, *Lamna ditropis*, lives along northern Pacific shores from Japan to northern California. Common thresher sharks are found in coastal waters on either side of the North Atlantic Ocean and among islands of the western and central Pacific Ocean, including Australia. There are two other species, the big-eyed thresher *(Alopias superciliosus)*, widespread in all the tropical and subtropical oceans, and pelagic threshers *(Alopias pelagicus)* of the Indian and western Pacific Oceans. Short-finned mako sharks occur in surface waters of all the world's oceans. Closely related long-finned mako sharks *(Isurus paucus)* live only in the Pacific Ocean.

■ Salmon sharks
□ Porbeagles

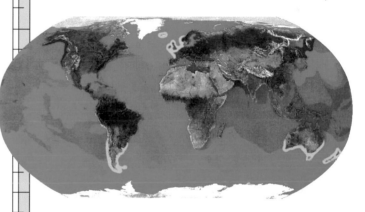

RELATIONSHIPS

In Greek mythology, Lamia was a horrible, man-eating monster. The name (slightly altered to Lamna) became the scientific name given to porbeagle sharks, and from them to the order Lamniformes. This includes the porbeagles together with several other monster sharks. Why are they called mackerel sharks? Mackerel are small fish that form enormous shoals close inshore in spring and summer. Fishermen knew that when the mackerel were about, dozens of these big sharks would soon come along to feed on them. There are about 16 different kinds of mackeral sharks, divided into seven families. In this book, in addition to the sharks on these pages, we have already met three species—great white sharks (pages 8–9), and basking and megamouth sharks (pages 28–29). There are more of these big, surface-living sharks on the next two pages (32–33).

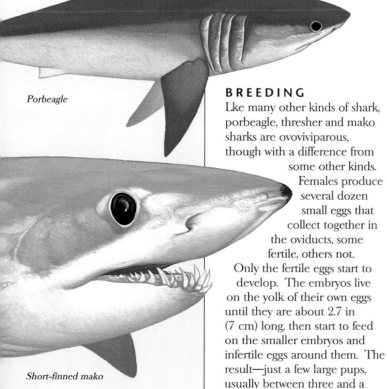

Porbeagle

Short-finned mako

MACKEREL SHARKS

2. More mackerel sharks: sand tiger, goblin and crocodile sharks, and the great white shark (pictured on pages 8–9).

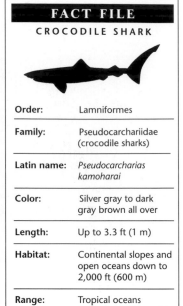
SAND TIGER SHARKS belong to the family Odontaspidae (o-dont-as-**pid**-ee), which in Greek means "rugged-toothed." These are large, heavyweight sharks with big mouths and a wall of tall spiky teeth, made up of three rows in each jaw. They swim with their mouths open, probably to make sure that they take in plenty of water and oxygen. This makes them look very fierce. Divers who see them approaching with open jaws begin to feel threatened, so sand tiger sharks have gained a reputation as man-hunters. In fact, like other mackerel sharks, they feed mostly on fish and squid, and usually keep well away from humans.

They spend most of their time near the bottom of shallow sandy bays, lagoons and reefs, sometimes in deeper water on undersea slopes. Divers often see them near the seabed in groups of several dozen, perhaps where food fish are gathering to breed. Like other sharks, they are sensitive to blood in the water and to the flapping movements of wounded fish. They have been known to swim up and steal fish caught on lines, so fishermen are seldom pleased when groups of sand tiger sharks move in.

Goblin sharks are mysterious deep-water fish with a strange, pointed shield overhanging their jaws, and an unusually flexible mouth. The first specimens were caught off Japan in the late 1800s.

Crocodile shark

Goblin shark

But their Y-shaped teeth were already known from fossil deposits, more than 100,000 years old, in places as far apart as England and Australia. Today, goblin sharks still seem to be widespread, living in mid-waters of warm and tropical seas, though they are probably quite rare. They have been caught well below surface waters in both the Atlantic and the Indian Oceans, as well as the Pacific, and seem to feed mainly on fish and squid. We know very little of how they live.

Crocodile sharks take their name from their large, "grinning" mouths and long, very sharp spiny teeth. They are the smallest mackerel sharks, only about 3.3 ft (1 m) long, with sleek bodies and large tails, suggesting they can swim fast. They also have unusually large eyes, which probably help them to see in poor light, both in mid-water where they spend most of their day, and near the surface where they hunt at night. Crocodile sharks are widespread in all the warm oceans and not uncommon. They feed on fish, squid and crustaceans, but we know very little else about them.

BREEDING

Sand tiger sharks, like other mackerel sharks, are ovoviviparous. Each female produces several eggs, keeping them in the oviducts. As those that are fertile develop, the embryos that grow quickest soon absorb their own yolk sacs. They start to eat both the smaller embryos and the unfertilized eggs that the mother continues to produce. In these species, only one embryo survives in each of the two oviducts, so only two pups are born at a time. Crocodile sharks have a similar way of breeding but manage to produce two pups from each oviduct, or four in a litter. Goblin sharks may well breed in the same way.

Sand tiger shark

Where do we find them?

Spotted sand tiger sharks are found in warm coastal and offshore waters on both sides of the Atlantic Ocean, in the Mediterranean Sea, along the south and east African coasts, and in the western Pacific Ocean. Goblin sharks have been caught in deep water (and occasionally in shallows) off Japan, Portugal and Australia and in the Indian Ocean, so are probably to be found in all the oceans. Crocodile sharks, too, occur in all the warm oceans, hunting near the surface at night and in deeper waters by day. Great white sharks occur in temperate waters of the Pacific, Indian and Atlantic Oceans.

███ Great white sharks

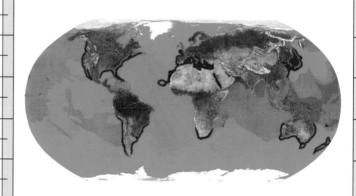

GREAT WHITE SHARKS

Great white sharks are also mackerel sharks. (For Fact File and picture, see pages 8–9.) They are generally similar to makos, though big ones grow very much bigger and heavier. They live in temperate to warm seas, usually over the continental shelf or among islands. They swim constantly and eat hungrily to maintain the necessary energy levels. Their mouths, with rows of triangular, saw-edged teeth, are always open. Great white sharks eat large fish, dolphins, seals and sea lions, and they have a well-deserved reputation for man-eating.

Great white shark—one of the longest mackerel sharks

RELATIONSHIPS

The three kinds of lamniform, or mackerel, sharks pictured left represent three different families. There are four species (some biologists say only three) of sand tiger sharks, all rather similar. The spotted, or common, one shown here is the most widespread. They are in many ways similar to mako and great white sharks, though less lively. Their two dorsal fins are more equal in size, and they have much larger anal fins. The strange-looking goblin sharks and crocodile sharks are grouped as mackerel sharks too, though they live in deeper water and are different in several ways from their more typical cousins. There is only one kind of each, and each forms a separate family on its own.

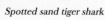

Spotted sand tiger shark

FACT FILE

SMALL-SPOTTED CAT SHARK

Order:	Carcharhiniformes
Family:	Scyliorhinidae (cat sharks)
Latin name:	*Scyliorhinus canicula*
Color:	Brownish gray with small dark spots above, paler underneath
Length:	Up to 3.3 ft (1 m)
Habitat:	Seabed in shallow temperate waters
Range:	Eastern North Atlantic Ocean, Mediterranean Sea

TOPE SHARK

Order:	Carcharhiniformes
Family:	Triakidae (houndsharks)
Latin name:	*Galeorhinus galeus*
Color:	Gray brown above, paler underneath
Length:	Up to 6.5 ft (2 m)
Habitat:	Continental shelves and slopes in temperate waters
Range:	Eastern Pacific Ocean

SNAGGLETOOTH SHARK

Order:	Carcharhiniformes
Family:	Hemigaleidae (weasel sharks)
Latin name:	*Hemipristis elongatus*
Color:	Gray or brown above, paler below
Length:	Up to 8 ft (2.5 m)
Habitat:	Shallow coastal waters of tropical seas down to 100 ft (30 m)
Range:	Eastern Atlantic Ocean, western Indian and Pacific Oceans

Gulf cat shark of Flinders Island, Australia

GROUND SHARKS

1. Cat sharks, houndsharks and weasel sharks. The biggest group of sharks and the most varied, ground sharks are found in all the world's oceans.

GROUND SHARKS ARE THE BIGGEST and most varied group of sharks, appearing in all the world's oceans from cool temperate to tropical regions. They have two dorsal fins without spines, an anal fin and usually a large mouth with rows of sharp teeth. The lower eyelids half-close when they are swallowing

different kinds have already been identified, and there are probably more still to be found. They live on the seabed, some in shallow water, though mostly in the deeper waters of the continental slopes, down to 6,500 ft (2,000 m). Many of the shallow-water species are brown or gray, with spots and patches that help them to match their background. They feed by grubbing about on the seafloor, digging out worms, shrimps, mussels, clams and other invertebrates.

Small-spotted cat shark

Tope shark

Snaggletooth shark

food, possibly to protect the eyes. Many of them, like the ones on these pages, are 3.3–8 ft (1–2.5 m) long, dark colored, and mottled or spotted to match the seabed.

Cat sharks are commonest of all the sharks. They are usually long and slender, with a broad, flat head and large spiracles just behind the eyes. Their name comes from the eyes, which are often yellow or green like a cat's eyes, with a narrow slit pupil. About 100

Tope sharks belong to a family of long, slender hunters called houndsharks. They live along coasts and over continental slopes in temperate and tropical seas. Topes are also called school sharks, because they tend to gather in groups, or schools, of up to 20–30. Banding together may help them to round up their prey, which are usually fish, squid and octopus. Another name for them is "soupfin shark," because their fins can be boiled to make a gelatinous soup. But this is true of many other species too.

Though large and fierce-looking, tope sharks are actually rather timid. Divers can seldom get near enough to photograph them or study their behavior. Inshore fishermen catch them for their skin, meat and fins. Individuals are known to travel long distances—for example, from Britain to Iceland, or along the west coast of America.

Snaggletooth sharks belong to the small, inshore family called weasel sharks, and live mainly in warm waters of the Indian and western Pacific Oceans. Usually uniform brown or gray, they are named for the large, saw-edged teeth of their lower jaw, which help them to grab and hold their prey, mainly schooling fish, which they hunt in shallow waters.

BREEDING

Cat sharks gather in huge shallow-water groups to mate. Females lay eggs with horny green or brown shells, which harden when they emerge into the sea. Tendrils at each corner attach them to rocks and seaweeds, where they remain almost invisible for several months before hatching. Tope sharks are ovoviviparous, laying as many as 50 eggs that remain in the uterus. The pups hatch, growing to lengths of about 1 ft (30 cm) before being born.

Mothers probably breed every two or three years. Snaggletooth sharks are viviparous, producing their young alive, though in a slightly different way that makes them seem more like mammals than fish. Females produce seven or eight eggs without shells, which remain in the uterus. After mating, the yolk sac of each egg attaches itself to the wall of the uterus, which is well supplied with blood. For the next few months the mother's bloodstream provides the embryos with all the nourishment they need to grow.

Epaulette cat shark, so-called from the dark shoulder patches

Where do we find them?

Ground sharks, the largest group of sharks, are also the most widespread, occurring in cold, temperate and warm seas all over the world. Catsharks generally have a worldwide distribution, though the small-spotted cat sharks shown here occur mainly in the north-eastern Atlantic and Mediterranean Sea. Tope sharks occur along the western shores of North America and Europe, the east coast of South America, around southern Africa and in Australian and New Zealand waters. Snaggletooth sharks occur in eastern Atlantic coastal waters, along the east coast of Africa, and among islands of the western Pacific Ocean.

COMMON NAMES
Common names for fish can be very confusing. The species of cat shark shown left is properly called the "small-spotted cat shark" because of its many small brown spots. However, fishermen off western Europe who catch many thousands of them each year, and traders who buy them for turning into fish meal, call them "common dogfish," or just "dogfish," because they are similar to the dogfish sharks (pp. 20–21) that they catch and use in the same way. That is why scientists try always to identify species by their scientific name, in this case *Scyliorhinus canicula*.

Tope sharks
Small-spotted cat sharks

Coral cat shark of Indonesia

RELATIONSHIPS

More than half the different kinds of sharks in the world belong to this group, the carcharhiniformes. They are commonly called "ground sharks" because many of them, like the ones shown here, live on or near the seabed. These are small- to medium-sized sharks that feed on invertebrates and fish from the seafloor, and are not particularly active or dangerous to man. But the group includes also some of the biggest, fiercest and most dangerous sharks of shallow coastal waters and mid-ocean, some of which appear on the following pages.

GROUND SHARKS

2. Requiem sharks—blue sharks, bull sharks, tigers and bronze whalers—fierce and dangerous predators that inhabit the world's tropical oceans.

FACT FILE	
BLUE SHARK	
Order:	Carcharhiniformes
Family:	Carcharhinidae (requiem sharks)
Latin name:	*Prionace glauca*
Color:	Dark blue above, shading to pale blue and white below
Length:	Up to 13 ft (4 m)
Habitat:	Open tropical oceans
Range:	Worldwide

BULL SHARK	
Order:	Carcharhiniformes
Family:	Carcharhinidae (requiem sharks)
Latin name:	*Carcharhinus leucas*
Color:	Gray brown above, paler below
Length:	Up to 11.5 ft (3.5 m)
Habitat:	Continental coasts, rivers and lakes
Range:	Worldwide in tropical and subtropical oceans

TIGER SHARK	
Order:	Carcharhiniformes
Family:	Carcharhinidae (requiem sharks)
Latin name:	*Galeocerdo cuvier*
Color:	Gray brown, striped when young, paler underneath
Length:	Up to 23 ft (7 m)
Habitat:	Coral reefs and tropical coasts, down to 500 ft (150 m)
Range:	Worldwide in tropical oceans

BRONZE WHALER SHARK	
Order:	Carcharhiniformes
Family:	Carcharhinidae (requiem sharks)
Latin name:	*Carcharinus brachyurus*
Color:	Brown or golden above, white below
Length:	Up to 10 ft (3 m)
Habitat:	Warm coastal and continental shelf waters
Range:	South Atlantic, eastern Pacific and western Indian Oceans

IF YOU SWIM IN WARM OR TROPICAL WATERS and are looking to lose a leg, these are the sharks to swim with. All four species have been involved in incidents in which swimmers have been attacked or killed. Never swim on your own if they are likely to be around. Be sure you are with people who know the dangers. The best advice is, if they are in the water, keep out.

Blue sharks are perhaps the most beautiful of all sharks. Dark blue above and pale blue to white below, shaped like elegant, streamlined aircraft, they glide through the water almost invisibly.

They are found most often in warm or tropical oceanic waters far from land, but also come close inshore—for example, among the islands of the Caribbean Sea. Individuals travel long distances across the oceans, following the currents in their constant search for food. They feed mainly on shoaling fish, but have also been seen to feed on dead whales and other carcasses. Of the four sharks shown here, they are probably the least likely to attack man, except by accident when they are hunting for other kinds of food.

Bull sharks are burly gray sharks, blunt-nosed, with small piggy eyes and a large, pointed dorsal fin, usually found along warm continental coasts. They are unusual in entering rivers and coastal lagoons, and swimming far up into freshwater, where they seem perfectly at home.

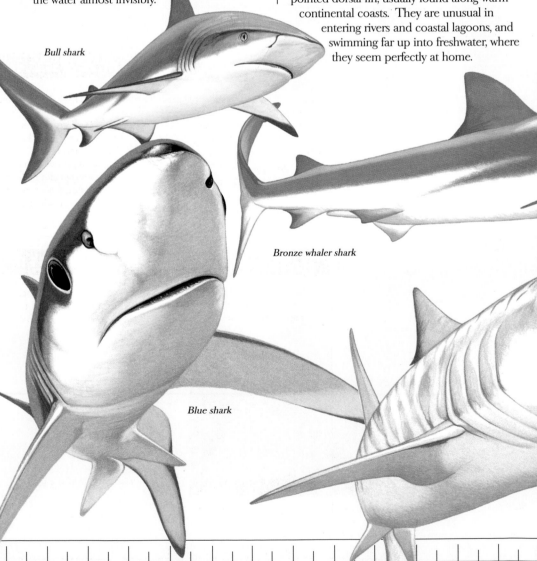

Bull shark

Bronze whaler shark

Blue shark

Bull sharks from the Gulf of Mexico have been found more than 1,000 miles (1,600 km) up the Mississippi River. Those from the Caribbean Sea swim far up the muddy waters of the Amazon River, and find their way through the swiftly flowing Río San Juan to the Lago de Nicaragua, a freshwater lake far inland. These are fierce sharks with an appetite for fish, porpoises and dolphins, turtles and carcasses. They have a well-established reputation as man-eaters.

Tiger sharks are so-called because the young ones have distinctive dark gray stripes, which tend to disappear as they grow older. When the stripes are no longer visible, the huge mouth, chunky barrel body and tapering tail help to distinguish them from other species. Their teeth are unique—asymmetrical and razor sharp. Tiger sharks are found in all tropical and subtropical oceans, though they are by no means common. Often they patrol off coral reefs, coming inshore when hungry to search for food. They eat large fish, turtles, porpoises and seals. Divers regard them as highly dangerous.

Bronze whaler sharks gained their name from their golden-brown color and their habit of attacking and tearing pieces from the carcasses of harpooned whales. They live in many warm coastal areas, where they feed mainly on shoaling fish caught in surface waters or near the seabed. But they also attack larger fish, and many have been known to attack bathers.

Gray reef shark

BREEDING
Tiger sharks are ovoviviparous, laying eggs that are retained and hatch in the uterus. Several dozen are produced at a time, so as many as 50 or more young sharks, each about 1.8–2 ft (50–60 cm) long, may emerge as a litter. Blue, bull and bronze whaler sharks are viviparous, producing many eggs which hatch inside the fish and attach themselves, by the yolk sac, to the wall of the uterus. There they develop for up to a year. As many as 100 small shark pups may be produced at a time.

Tiger shark

Where do we find them?

The bigger the species of shark, the more likely it is to roam widely across the world's oceans. These are all big sharks, with wide geographical ranges. They follow the surface currents in circular tracks that may eventually lead them back to where they began. Blue and tiger sharks are most widespread in the open oceans, tiger sharks mostly in the warmer tropics, blue sharks in cooler tropical and warm temperate seas. Blue sharks occasionally visit as far north as Britain and New England, and in the south are regular visitors to New Zealand's South Island. Bull sharks appear worldwide in coastal regions, and also enter estuaries and rivers. Bronze whalers have a slightly more restricted coastal distribution.

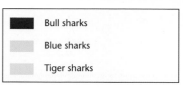

■ Bull sharks

▨ Blue sharks

▨ Tiger sharks

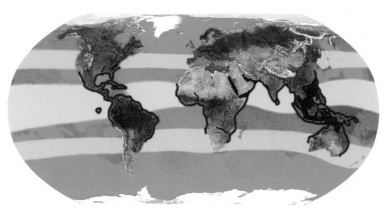

RELATIONSHIPS

These four sharks belong to the family called requiem sharks. "Requiem" means "rest," and some say these sharks were so-named because they appear most often when the sea is calm. Others link the name with the "requiem mass," a religious service for the dead. For them requiem is a grim reminder that these sharks are big enough, and often hungry enough, to kill and eat people. There are between 40 and 50 species in the family. Though not all are man-eaters, many are big enough to tackle the biggest bony fish and have no difficulty in taking human swimmers close to the shore.

TEETH

Requiem sharks all have rows of razor-sharp enameled teeth, set firmly in the skin that grows from their gums. In several species these have distinctive shapes. Victims of shark attack seldom know what species attacked them, but the tooth marks, and fragments of teeth left in the wounds, are sometimes useful aids to identification.

BULL   **BRONZE**   **TIGER**   **BLUE**

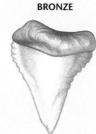

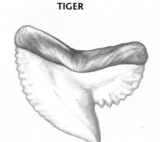

FACT FILE

SMOOTH HAMMERHEAD SHARK

Order:	Carcharhiniformes
Family:	Sphyrnidae
Latin name:	*Sphyrna zygaena*
Color:	Gray green above, white underneath
Length:	Up to 11.5 ft (3.5 m)
Habitat:	Inshore and shelf waters down to 1,000 ft (300 m)
Range:	North Atlantic, western Indian and Pacific Oceans

BONNET SHARK

Order:	Carcharhiniformes
Family:	Sphyrnidae
Latin name:	*Sphyrna tiburo*
Color:	Gray green above, white underneath
Length:	3.3 ft (1 m)
Habitat:	Inshore areas from surf down to 330 ft (100 m)
Range:	Western Atlantic and eastern Pacific Oceans

WINGHEAD SHARK

Order:	Carcharhiniformes
Family:	Sphyrnidae
Latin name:	*Sphyrna blochii*
Color:	Gray green above, white underneath
Length:	Up to 5 ft (1.5 m)
Habitat:	Inshore and shelf waters
Range:	Eastern Indian and southwestern Pacific Oceans

GREAT HAMMERHEAD SHARK

Order:	Carcharhiniformes
Family:	Sphyrnidae
Latin name:	*Sphyrna mokarran*
Color:	Gray green above, white underneath
Length:	Up to 16.5 ft (5 m)
Habitat:	Inshore and shelf waters down to 330 ft (100 m)
Range:	North Atlantic, western Indian and eastern Pacific Oceans

GROUND SHARKS

3. The hammerhead sharks—bonnet and winghead sharks, smooth and great hammerhead sharks—nightmare creatures with eyes on extensions of their head.

LOOK AT ANY OF THESE FISH from the side and they seem perfectly normal—beautifully streamlined sharks with tapered heads, two dorsal fins and a single anal fin. The big, sail-like front dorsal fins and large tails suggest speed and power. But see them from above and they are like nothing else on earth. The heads are expanded on either side, as though pressed by a heavy roller. The eyes are spaced on the very tips of the expansions, and nostril grooves run the length of the leading edges.

These are the hammerhead sharks. The bonnet sharks are closest to the normal shark pattern, relatively small, with a flattened, disk-shaped head in which eyes and nostrils appear on the very edges of the disk. The smooth hammerhead is an intermediate form, growing much larger, with a broader, more hammer-shaped head. The winghead and great hammerhead represent extremes. Wingheads are relatively small sharks with enormous heads —the head from eye to eye is almost half the length of the body. Great hammerheads are big sharks, 13 ft (4 m) or more in length, with square-cut hammer-shaped head over 3.3 ft (1 m) wide. If you met one in a nightmare, you would probably be glad to wake up.

Why these curious shapes? We do not know, but we can guess at some of the advantages. The bonnet and the hammerhead have shapes that, as the shark glides through the sea, help to lift the front end of the body. The flat heads may make it easier for the sharks to turn and twist in the water. Having the eyes set so far apart may help them to judge distance more clearly. Hammerheads are known to have a keen sense of smell. The long grooves diverting water from the ends of the wings to the nostrils may allow them to check a wider sample as they pass through the water. Hammerhead sharks have more electrosensory organs on their skin (see "Electrodetectors," opposite page) than most other sharks. A row of these across the broad front of the head may scan a wider swath of the seabed in front of them.

Hammerhead sharks are lively, fast-moving sharks, most of them medium-sized (up to 6.5 ft, or 2 m, long). The smaller ones feed on

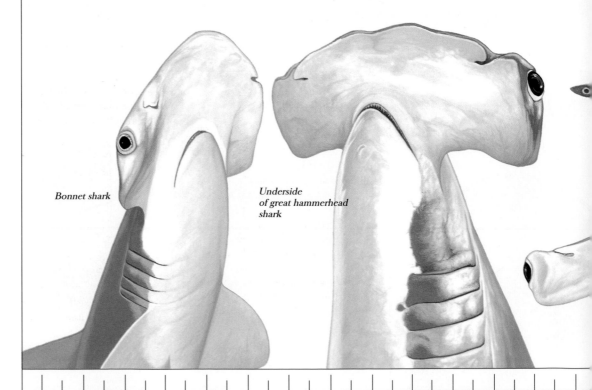

Bonnet shark

Underside of great hammerhead shark

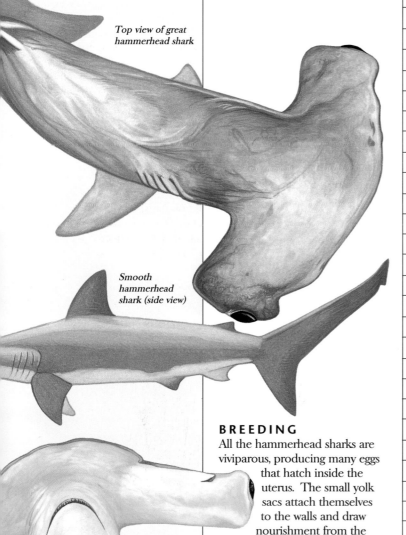

small fish, squid, octopus and invertebrates rustled up from the seafloor. The bigger ones feed on shoaling fish and often tackle such big fish as skates and rays, including electric rays.

Big hammerheads are dangerous to man. If you are swimming and one comes around, don't stop to admire it. Get out of the water as soon as you can.

Top view of great hammerhead shark

Smooth hammerhead shark (side view)

Winghead shark

ELECTRO-DETECTORS

Many kinds of sharks have rows of sensory organs under the skin of their flanks and head (see p. 15). These organs are called "ampullae of Lorenzini" after the Italian scientist who first described them more than 300 years ago. They are sensitive to low-frequency sounds and small electric currents, of a kind that fish and other living creatures give off whenever they move or change position. Hammerhead sharks, like other lively, active predators, are particularly well equipped with these organs, which probably help them to find and pinpoint fish, such as skates and rays, that are half-buried in sand or mud.

BREEDING

All the hammerhead sharks are viviparous, producing many eggs that hatch inside the uterus. The small yolk sacs attach themselves to the walls and draw nourishment from the mother's bloodstream. It takes up to a year for them to develop, and several dozen pups are born at a time.

Where do we find them?

Hammerhead sharks live in all the temperate, warm and tropical oceans. Bonnet sharks are found along eastern Pacific Ocean shores from southern California to Ecuador, and along western Atlantic shores from South Carolina to southern Brazil. Smooth hammerheads roam warm temperate and tropical coasts on either side of the North Atlantic Ocean and the western Indian Ocean, and throughout the Pacific Ocean. Great hammerheads have a similar distribution but are restricted to the eastern Pacific Ocean. Wingheads are found mainly among the islands and peninsulas of Southeast Asia, and in the Persian Gulf.

| ■ | Bonnet sharks | ▢ | Smooth hammerhead sharks |
| ▢ | Winghead sharks | ▢ | Great hammerhead sharks |

RELATIONSHIPS

There are nine species of sharks with these curious and unique shapes of head. Their bodies make it clear that they belong to the largest order of sharks, the Carcharhiniformes, but the head shapes make them quite different from all other sharks. We call them hammerhead sharks, and place them in a family of their own, the Sphyrnidae (pronounce it **sfer**-nid-ee). The four species shown here illustrate the range of head shapes within the group, from the bonnet shark's flat, round head with eyes spaced far apart, to the great hammerhead's extreme flat rectangle, with eyes far out on the sides.

Great hammerhead shark

FACT FILE

MANTA RAY

Order:	Batoidei
Family:	Mobulidae
Latin name:	*Manta birostris*
Color:	Black or dark gray above, pale below
Length:	Up to 40 ft (12 m)
Habitat:	Surface tropical waters
Range:	All the tropical oceans

ATLANTIC GUITARFISH

Order:	Hypotremata
Family:	Rhinobatidae
Latin name:	*Rhinobatos lentiginosus*
Color:	Gray or brown with white spots above, pale fawn below
Length:	Up to 2.5 ft (75 cm)
Habitat:	Shallow coastal waters
Range:	Western Atlantic coast, North Carolina to Mexico

COMMON SKATE

Order:	Hypotremata
Family:	Rajidae
Latin name:	*Raia batis*
Color:	Gray brown with pale spots above, paler below
Length:	Up to 6.5 ft (2 m)
Habitat:	Shallow water seabed
Range:	Northeastern Atlantic Ocean

ELECTRIC RAY

Order:	Batoidei
Family:	Torpedinidae
Latin name:	*Torpedo torpedo*
Color:	Reddish brown with blue eyespots above, pale below
Length:	Up to 2 ft (60 cm)
Habitat:	Sandy or gravel seabed
Range:	Warm temperate European coasts

SKATES AND RAYS

Close relations of the sharks, these gristle fish are shaped for life on the seabed as well as on the ocean surface.

THE GUITARFISH, so-called from their body shape, seem to be halfway between sharks and skates. From above, the front half of their body is kite-shaped, with lateral "wings" made up of huge pectoral fins extending right to the front of the head. The pelvic fins form secondary wings, with a thin, sharklike tail, mounting two dorsal fins, extending behind. These fish take in water through their spiracles, set just behind the eyes, and pass it out through the gill slits on their underside. The teeth are flat, for crushing rather than cutting.

They feed mainly on shellfish, shrimps, crabs and small fish, which they catch by stalking and pouncing upon on the seafloor. There are between 40 and 50 species, all found in warm shallow waters. The biggest grow to 6 ft (2 m) long.

The skates seem to have taken flattening and broadening a stage further. As in guitarfish, their pectoral fins and pelvic fins have become lateral "wings," but the "kite" is bigger, the tail much thinner, and the dorsal fins reduced to small stumps.

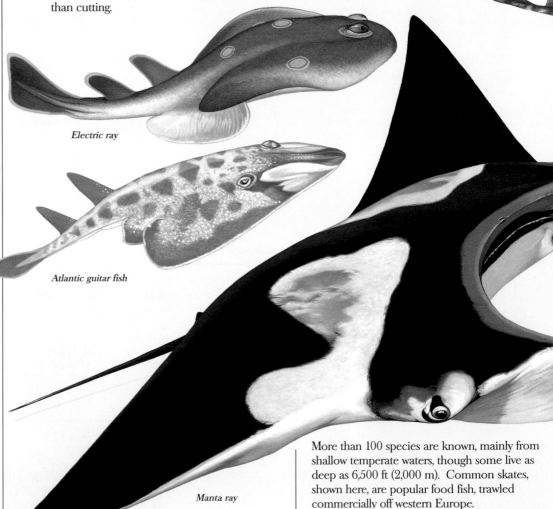

Electric ray

Atlantic guitar fish

Manta ray

More than 100 species are known, mainly from shallow temperate waters, though some live as deep as 6,500 ft (2,000 m). Common skates, shown here, are popular food fish, trawled commercially off western Europe.

Rays come in all shapes and sizes. Some live almost entirely on the seabed, others almost entirely in surface waters. Some, the stingrays, carry one or two spines at the base of their tails that inject a painful poison. Take care if you are walking in shallows along warm subtropical coasts. Walking barefoot is fun, but it is safer to wear shoes. You will know immediately if you tread on a sting ray. The sting can be very painful and may last several days.

Electric rays have spines that give a mild electric shock, paralyzing to other fish, but only mildly numbing to humans. There are about 35 species, living mainly in warm shallow waters. Their electricity is produced in muscular "batteries" on either side of the head. You feel the shock if you touch their surface. They use electric shocks probably to

Skate

scare off predators, but also to stun prey fish before grabbing and eating them. The species shown here is a small one. Others grow to 8 ft (2.5 m) or more.

Manta rays spend all their time swimming, seldom if ever touching the seabed. "Manta" is Spanish for "blanket"—these huge fish must have reminded early sailors of a blanket floating in the water. There are over a dozen species, the smallest less than 3.3 ft (1 m) long, the largest possibly up to 50 ft (15 m) long.

Among the weirdest fish in the oceans, the big mantas are also called "sea bats" or "eagle rays" because of their flapping wings, or "sea devils" because of their frightening size and appearance. In fact, like the biggest sharks, manta rays are relatively harmless, feeding mostly on shrimps and shoaling fish. Divers sometimes take rides on them, holding on to their "horns" or tail.

BREEDING

Atlantic guitarfish are ovoviviparous, breeding yearly. Five or six eggs are incubated within the oviduct until they hatch, and the mothers give birth immediately.

Stingray

Other, larger species of guitarfish probably produce more at a time. Electric rays breed in a very similar way, producing litters of about a dozen newly hatched young. Skate lay eggs, usually rectangular, in black or dark gray horny cases with tendrils at the corners. You can often pick up the empty cases along the beach.

Manta rays give birth to just one or two large, well-developed pups at a time. The newborn pup of a large manta may be 5 ft (1.5 m) long at birth.

Where do we find them?

Like sharks, the skates and rays are found in all the world's oceans. Most of the bottom-living forms are coastal or live in deeper waters on the continental slopes. The three bottom-living species shown here are typical in not having very wide distributions, but there are many closely related species of guitarfish, skates and electric rays in similar areas elsewhere in the world. Only the manta rays have wide distributions, appearing in all the tropical oceans

■	Atlantic guitarfish
▨	Manta ray
▨	Common skate

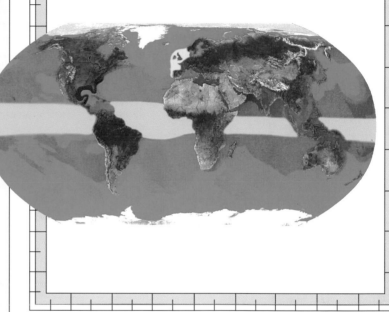

FLYING MANTAS

Throughout the ages manta rays have frightened fishermen by leaping and somersaulting out of the water alongside their boats, and returning with a huge splash. This makes a thunderous noise and dangerous waves, enough to upset a small boat. We do not know why they do this, but you sometimes see a dozen or more playing and leaping together, so it is likely to form part of courtship or threat display.

School of bat rays, closely related to manta rays

RELATIONSHIPS

Closely related to the sharks, and just as diverse and widespread, the skates and rays are gristle fish that live all the world over. Basically they are sharks whose ancestors settled for life on the seabed, and over many millions of years have grown flatter and flatter. This makes it easier for them to blend with their background, to lie in wait for prey and to hide from predators. Some have found that their flat, kitelike shape helps them to swim in surface waters too. All the skates and rays swim well, but the mantas and others like them spend most of their time swimming at or near the surface.

ARE SHARKS DANGEROUS TO HUMANS?

Here are some points to think about:

- Most sharks are too small and too timid or live too deep in the ocean to be of any danger to humans
- No sharks anywhere in the world depend for their living on hunting people
- So long as we remain on land, no shark can touch us
- Only when we enter the sea, which is the sharks' world, do we put ourselves in danger from sharks
- Millions of swimmers and divers enter the sea every year, enjoy their swim and come out safely
- Just a few people every year are bitten or killed by sharks
- Swimmers are usually taken on beaches where, from time to time, big sharks are known to swim
- Swimmers who are bitten have usually been taking a known risk —and lost
- More people are killed on roads in a month than have been killed by sharks in a century

Gray nurse shark

In South Africa, the southern United States, Australia and other places where dangerous sharks are likely to appear, there are several ways of reducing risks of shark attacks:

- steel nets to keep the sharks away from beaches
- spotter aircraft flying overhead, looking for sharks in the water
- observation towers, with guards keeping a close eye on swimmers

DANGEROUS SHARKS AND SHARKS IN DANGER

Certain sharks have reputations as man-eaters, but sharks are far more endangered by humans.

Between human and shark, there can be no doubt as to which is more dangerous to the other. Every year, just a few dozen people are bitten by sharks. Every year, several tens or hundreds of thousands of sharks, along with thousands more skates and rays, are caught and killed by humans in nets or on hooks.

Most of the sharks caught are entirely harmless. Several thousand are killed each year for sport, by fishermen who want to test their strength and skill against that of a shark. However, many tens or hundreds of thousands more are taken in trawl nets or hooked individually by commercial fishermen.

Bringing in makos

Here are some of their uses:

- **meat**—for human food, pet food and meal for animal feed and fertilizers
- **fins**—for soup
- **livers**—for oil (lubricants, cosmetics) and vitamin extraction
- **blood, eyes, cartilage and other tissues**—for medical purposes
- **skin**—for leather and abrasives
- **teeth**—for jewelry

Sharks have been hunted for centuries, though usually in numbers small enough for them to survive without difficulty. Today, both sport and commercial fishing have increased to the point where many local stocks of small sharks, and some species of big ones, are becoming scarce.

Sharks dangerous to humans

SAVING THE SHARK

Among the thousands of nature-lovers who support campaigns to save whales, seals and birds from harm, you would find relatively few who would be willing to save sharks—or were even aware that some species of sharks are in need of protection. This is a pity. Sharks in their own way are no less magnificent than whales, and some may be even more in need of our care. If you are interested in sharks, and would like to help, try to contact one or more of the organizations listed on page 45.

Butchered sharks

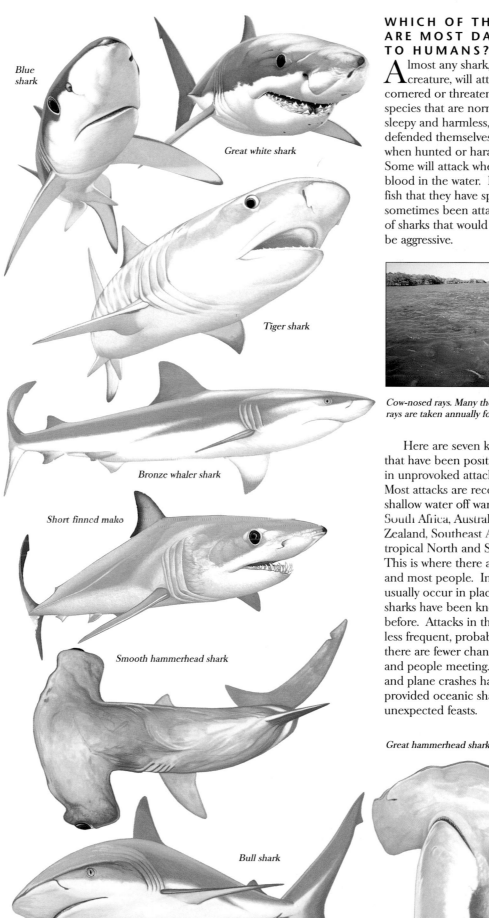

Blue shark

Great white shark

Tiger shark

Bronze whaler shark

Short finned mako

Smooth hammerhead shark

Bull shark

WHICH OF THE SHARKS ARE MOST DANGEROUS TO HUMANS?

Almost any shark, like any other creature, will attack if cornered or threatened. Some species that are normally timid, or sleepy and harmless, have defended themselves by attacking when hunted or harassed by divers. Some will attack when there is blood in the water. Divers carrying fish that they have speared have sometimes been attacked by kinds of sharks that would not normally be aggressive.

Cow-nosed rays. Many thousands of rays are taken annually for food

Here are seven kinds of sharks that have been positively identified in unprovoked attacks on humans. Most attacks are recorded in shallow water off warm beaches of South Africa, Australia, New Zealand, Southeast Asia, and tropical North and South America. This is where there are most sharks and most people. Incidents usually occur in places where sharks have been known to attack before. Attacks in the open sea are less frequent, probably because there are fewer chances of sharks and people meeting. Shipwrecks and plane crashes have sometimes provided oceanic sharks with unexpected feasts.

Great hammerhead shark

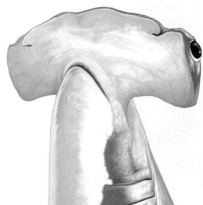

GLOSSARY

Can you identify the species pictured?
(answers below)

abdomen	Stomach
adapt	To change (something) to make better or more efficient
aggressive	Likely to attack
barbel	Fleshy strand hanging from the skin. Some are sensitive to touch or scent, others are for decoration or protection
carnivore	Animal that feeds mainly on the flesh of other animals
cloaca	Hole in the body wall through which pass feces (food waste), urine (waste from kidneys), eggs and newborn young
conservation	Saving and protecting species, usually by protecting the places where they live
density	Number (of animals) in a particular area
digestive system	Parts of an animal in which food is broken down and absorbed (mouth, throat, stomach, intestines, etc.)
dominant	Most important; able to control others
forage	To search for food
fossil	Remnant of plant or animal preserved in stone
habitat	Place where a plant or animal lives
herbivore	Animal that feeds mainly on vegetation and plant life
invertebrates	Animals without a backbone, such as worms, crabs, shrimps, insects, spiders
larvae	Young forms of fish, insects, worms, shellfish, etc.
mid-water	Broad zone of the sea between surface and seabed
monitoring	Watching carefully to see what progress is being made
nutrients	Chemical components or parts of food that are essential to health
omnivore	Animal that eats both flesh and vegetation
oviduct	Passage in the female through which eggs are laid
oviparous	Egg-laying
ovoviviparous	Producing eggs that hatch within the mother, so the young are born alive
pelagic	Living at or near the sea surface
phytoplankton	Tiny plant cells drifting in surface waters of sea or lake; part of the plankton (see zooplankton)

From top: great white, broad-nosed seven-gilled, prickly, nurse

plankton	Tiny plants and animals drifting in surface waters of sea or lake (see phytoplankton, zooplankton)
population	Part of a species living in a particular area, sometimes but not always separated geographically from other populations of the same species (see stock)
predator	Animal that hunts and kills other animals for food
pregnant	Carrying a developing baby inside the body
prey	Animal that is hunted and killed by other animals
scavenge	To eat refuse or old food that has been lying around for some time
serrated	Sawlike
shoal (of fish)	Group of fish swimming together
spawning	Egg-laying
species	A particular kind of plant or animal
spiracle	Small gill slit immediately behind the eye
stock	Small group of animals or plants of one species forming part of a population (see population)
uterus	Part of the female reproductive organs where eggs and embryos develop
vertebrates	Animals with a backbone, including fishes, amphibians, reptiles, birds and mammals
viviparous	Producing live young that have drawn food from the wall of the uterus
zooplankton	Tiny animals (often including eggs and young forms of fish, worms, shellfish, etc.) drifting in surface waters of sea or lake; part of the plankton (see phytoplankton)

Useful addresses The Shark Trust, 36 Kingfisher Court, Hambridge Rd, Newbury, Berkshire RG14 5SJ, UK

Shark Research Institute, PO Box 50775, V&A Waterfront, Cape Town 8001, South Africa

Shark Specialist Group, Florida Museum of Natural History, University of Florida, Museum Rd., Gainesville, FL 32611

World Wildlife Fund, 1250 24th St. NW, Suite 500, Washington, DC 20037

American Elasmobranch Society, Department of Biology, University of Massachusetts, 385 Old Westport Rd., Dartmouth, MA 02747-2300

From top: bull, smooth hammerhead, basking, spotted sand tiger

INDEX